The LEAST of THESE

the Graham Staines Story

ANDREW E. MATTHEWS

a. Acorn Press

Published by Acorn Press
An imprint of Bible Society AustraliaACN 148 058 306
Charity licence 19 000 528
GPO Box 4161
Sydney NSW 2001
Australia
www.acornpress.net.au | www.biblesociety.org.au

ISBN 978-0-647-53348-2

First published by Tablo Publishing.
Second edition published by Morning Star Publishing in 2019,
ISBN 978-0-648-45381-9

Novella published with the permission of Gladys Staines.

Image courtesy of Sharman Joshi.

Film image courtesy of Skypass Entertainment India.
[Location: Araku Valley, Andhra Pradesh, India]

NATIONAL LIBRARY OF AUSTRALIA

A catalogue record for this work is available from the National Library of Australia

Cover design: JCNB
Typesetting: John Healy

Contents

AUTHOR'S NOTE

I have only gratitude to God and all those who have made possible the completion of the film and now the publication of this novella. Thank you.

In particular, I must thank my wife and children for their patience and support, Victor Abraham for his generosity and philanthropy, Aneesh Daniel for his vision and friendship, Krish Dhanam for his kindness and encouragement, and Gladys Staines for her resolute faithfulness.

I hope, dear Reader, that you will be moved by this story, feel for the character who tells it and see in your mind's eye something of the places and the people. Truth lies behind all that is fictionalised here. And that may cause you to ponder the tragedies and paradoxes of life, but also the hope and meaning and purpose that enables many to overcome.

Andrew E Matthews

FOREWORD

William Carey said that if we want to expect great things from God, we must attempt great things for God. Adoniram Judson said there can be no success without sacrifice. Both these men are regaled as heroes of the faith for their pioneering work in India and Burma (modern day Myanmar). Tucked away between the missionary zeal of those that went to fulfil the Great Commission and those that stayed to reveal the Great Commandment is the story of Graham and Gladys Staines. Their sacrifice was as great as any that answered the call and their love was similar to the saint of Calcutta Mother Teresa who lived five hours northeast of them.

This book takes you to the heart of their story. One that began a hundred plus years ago when missionaries came to the sleepy town of Baripada in the state of Orissa to uplift those cast away because of the scourge of leprosy. My dear friend Andrew Matthews who was instrumental in bringing the Staines story to the big screen with an amazing screenplay now takes you on the same journey in print. What unfolds in the pages ahead is an objective look at a subjective reality that engages us the reader on the trials and tribulations of the calling of a missionary and the obedience to "The Caller."

You will become familiar with a foreign landscape that challenges those that go and convinces those that stay of the fine line between the culture that defines man and the condition that determines them. In this game of give and take the scorecard is deceptive as the victory is an eternal reward. Yet the temporal struggle to stay the course while being a father and a husband becomes the foundation upon which the house and heed of God is built. I assure you that you will be intrigued by the decisions of some and inspired by the demands of others. *The Least of These* is told as a story but it is a window into reality that gives us the blessed assurance that because He lives we can face tomorrow. That is the anthem that sustained them and gave them the courage to believe that they could expect great things because they had attempted great things. You will be blessed by the way this story looks into the light, life and legacy of a family that realized that their success was indeed their sacrifice.

Krish Dhanam
Author and Speaker

PROLOGUE

Something happened today.

Something very small, something seemingly insignificant, yet something that sits me now at an old typewriter, tapping these words, typed letters appearing on the paper... for whom? For me? For you?

Earlier today I stood in front of a small bookshop on a street in Kolkata. I stood looking at a book, small and thin like the shop, cheaply bound. I stood looking at the cover on which was a picture of a man. A man I knew.

Once.

Above the man lies the title. Yes, I bought the book. I assume this title is a play on words... *Staines of India* - there was a man, Staines, and there were things that happened, things that are a stain on India.

I didn't know they were going to happen.

If I had known I would never have gone to Orissa with a heavily pregnant wife. Not that there were many alternatives... but I'm making excuses.

As Mishra pointed out, I was young and inexperienced. And foolish.

EMPLOYMENT

My dear, dedicated and cherished wife.

She was resting on our few belongings in the shade of a bus station building, her red saree like a *chaulai*, the only flower in a forgotten garden, a single spill of colour in the dry and dusty surroundings.

I approached from behind her, carrying two small symbols of extravagance, tiny gifts of celebration, or perhaps guilt offerings. I recall my insides tightened as she adjusted her position uncomfortably, one hand on her stomach, the other leaning heavily on the suitcase alongside her.

But I could envisage no alternative to our predicament. The promised garden of abundance was but a few straggly plants, the fruit of which was uncertain at best. How could I reveal the true gravity of our situation without causing distress?

No, I had to find the evidence Mishra wanted, that was all. I had to produce the material that would secure the job. Shanti did not need to know; it was kinder to leave her at peace than to burden her with my mistakes.

Forcing fear from me, focusing on what was needed, to provide a sense of hope and security, I stepped up quietly behind her, and slipped the small tray with its meagre offerings in front of her.

"Sweetmeats for the lady."

She did not disappoint; she never did. Her face laughing with delight, hands clasped together, she bestowed on me her treasured look of love and faith before tenderly reaching for the first of the sweets, holding it delicately, carefully, as if it were a far greater gift, a much more magnificent endowment than a mere morsel of food.

After the first tantalising taste had satisfied the baby's longing of sweet things, her eyes moved back to mine, without hint of fear or reprimand.

"Well?" she asked.

I pulled the camera from behind my back where it hung in its black case, letting her believe what she wanted, the camera providing a suitable alibi - I didn't need to say anything.

Her face beamed back at me and her hand closed on mine. Now she could savour her sweet in complete contentment.

"It's not much," I warned.

"It's a job."

I avoided her eyes, ostensibly looking at the bus signs.

"We're going to the town of Baripada. Not too far - a bus ride."

I didn't tell her it was a three hour ride on an over-crowded old bus with uncomfortable seating. It was hardly the moment to dump reality on her. That came soon enough.

The ride itself was uneventful. Uncomfortable for Shanti, uncomplaining as always, whereas for me it was a mixture of emotions - concern for Shanti, frustration with my shortcomings, excitement at the possibilities.

I confess the dominant feeling was excitement. The confidence and faith I had in my own abilities, misplaced of course, were re-asserting their rule over my general outlook. I knew I could do this. I had no reason to doubt that I would find the evidence Mishra was looking for - I had no experience to suggest otherwise. So, with the confidence of youth, I felt that it was only a matter of time, and a short time at that, before my position at the newspaper would be confirmed and Shanti's assumption would become reality.

I enjoyed the journey, infinitely more than the subsequent journeys I had to take on that same route, but I will come to some of those.

This one filled me with an immense sense of purpose. As I watched the land fade and disappear under the smoky haze into which we were travelling, the land cut into the myriad shapes of the drying paddies like a patchwork of garden beds, littered with mounds of cut rice, the odd pair of skinny bullocks pulling large-wheeled trays heaped high with the collected mounds, my spirit swelled with a sense of mission, a desire to protect and champion the rural way of life that was being eroded, a way of life I romantically thought close to the ideal.

In fact I had little idea of what that life was really like.

But as I watched the rice-paddied landscape, randomly ripped through by small waterways and inevitably interrupted by villages, congregations of the people who work and live off the land, I grew in my conviction that their traditions needed protecting against destructive western influences, the front line of which was represented by the Christian missionaries, one of whom I was to investigate and expose.

But how exactly did we come to be on a bus to Baripada?

I had recently completed my studies in Journalism and it was my desire for paid journalism work, mostly, that had brought me to Orissa. Earlier, while Shanti had waited at the bus station, I had been sitting in the office of one Roshan Mishra, a newspaper editor.

He was a round little man. I don't mean that in an insulting way; he just was. He was also critically important to me. I sat in his office, separated from him by an ocean- sized desk, varnished with a dark stain, the desk inundated with waves of papers.

I waited as calmly as I could while he looked again at my portfolio of articles and viewed recent photos I had taken of a clash between Hindu and Christian believers. The Christians had gathered in the centre of the village before marching to their church, singing and proselytizing. The offence was met by resistance. By the time they reached their church, men had gathered.

I had waited, hoping, as all journalists do.

And I was rewarded. The Christians tried to push through the group and a clash ensued. I got some good photos. Until they started beating the kids as well. I know a journalist is supposed to be impartial and simply observe, but the kids... perhaps something in my background, perhaps some innate personality twist - something in me baulks at blaming children for their parents' folly. I tried to stop the men. I had a sore head for days afterwards.

I also had sore emotions. The fools. I ask you - how did they think photos of them beating children was going to help their cause? And then beating the journalist who was helping them? If I had already been a paid journalist my writing would have punished them the very next day. As it was, I had time to calm down and realise that my hurt had to give way to the cause, especially the cause of securing a paid position.

I already had some good photos to support that cause and these were now spread across the desk, floating on the waves of paper, all my hope contained in Mishra's eyes as they darted between photos, his fat little hands - I mean no disrespect - snatching photos from the fleet and sliding them upside down into a pile at the point where his belly met the desk, apparently unsalvageable for the anticipated article.

I needed this job, badly. Competition for this kind of work is stiff in India - it's probably the same anywhere in the world. One needs family connections and money to keep you going while you build your portfolio and reputation. I had neither.

To be honest, I was taking the greatest risk of my life. We desperately needed money now. Our supply had run out, but rather than seek menial employment I had risked everything on Roshan Mishra coming through with the job he had promised in his letter.

'Promised' is perhaps too strong as the wording was vague, but that's what I told Shanti. He was certainly interested in employing me and had invited me to an interview, which he implied, was a mere formality. After all, I did have certain advantages. The newspaper he ran was state-based, but a large regional paper, printed in the Oriya language. Big enough to be a great start for a young journalist like myself. I had grown up with Oriya as a second language and good writing is good writing. I was proficient enough to reduce the competition in this region.

So there I was, having spent almost the last of our supply to get there, trying not to fidget or let on just how desperate I was. In India one needs bargaining power, and when bargaining, desperation is deadly. I was very conscious of my hands - I was all but sitting on them to keep them still. Be calm!

All the while the other hands, the god-like hands, with apparent arbitrary apathy snatched photos from the ocean desk. Would there be any left, I wondered?

The hands stilled above the few remaining scraps of hope, a stop in the storm. He looked up from the photos to me. I smiled, pretending confidence. His face was inscrutable, but I held my nerve... well, no, maybe not. The false smile was probably fastened to my face, revealing all.

The hands descended from the heavens once more, swooping up one of the last remaining... he flipped the photo around for me to see.

"This one."

My heart leapt. I think I held my breath, not sure whether he was asking a question or maybe, just maybe, thinking of actually using it and printing a story!

The photo was of a moment at the beginning of the clash where a man had grabbed the stick of his opponent with both hands and a struggle had followed. You couldn't tell who the attacker was.

"Christians defy Council ban," he stated.

And then, unbelievably, I lost my focus. Clearly he was implying that he could use the photo and I would write the article - I should have complimented him on a good choice and offered to write the article immediately, irrespective. Instead I sat with that foolish grin on my face, nodding my head, but at a complete loss as to how I would write such an article.

You see, in my panic I could not make the connection between the facts, being Christmas day and the Christians going to church, and the story about a Council ban that Mishra was apparently asking me to write.

They obviously did a better job of training me at Journalism School than I thought: 'objective journalist' was the catch cry.

"Well?" Mishra asked.

"Yes Sir," I answered pathetically. "How do you suggest I bring the Council ban in, Sir?

He was impatient.

"They were in a group?"

"Yes, Sir."

"Then they were marching without Council permission. That is enough. The violence that erupted was a direct result of this defiant action of theirs."

He spoke fast, watching me closely as he continued. I tried to look impressed at his logic as well as amused at how I could not have made such a logical connection myself. I am smart enough to know he was watching for body language, trying to come to a decision, perhaps even reconsidering a decision he had previously made.

My awareness that I had made a foolish mistake, that I had sailed my little boat called Hope straight back into the storm, did not help my confidence.

"We have a duty, as journalists," he continued, "to inform the public of what is really going on. What we see is not everything."

I was fully attentive now - the obedient student, in full agreement. I had to at least try to turn the impression of foolishness I had created.

"We have to delve," he continued, warming to his cause, "uncover the real motives behind the actions. American and European missionaries come over here, fly into a poor area in a helicopter, make great promises to the illiterate untouchables, promising gifts if they convert. And what does a conversion cost them?"

"Twelve dollars."

He nodded, I think a little pleased that I knew.

"Twelve dollars. And when they go back to America, having

washed their hands with disinfectant, they tell their people they had thousands of converts. And the people are so impressed they give them money, hundreds, thousands for each conversion. It's very good business."

He paused, turning to the window now and staring out over the sea of building block houses typical of Indian cities, as if he could see past them to the vast array of scattered humanity beyond, the rural villages of India.

"But here, back in the village, confusion. The new converts insult their neighbours. They no longer observe the age-old traditions, the festivals, the sacrifices. The people fear as a result that the land will not deliver its food or the rains won't come. Families are split apart. Societal disintegration."

I waited for him to turn, but he remained staring out into the distance. I didn't want to let the opportunity pass, so I spoke.

"I'm very much in agreement, Sir."

He turned back to the desk.

"The law states that no person shall convert another by force, allurement or fraudulent means."

He planted his finger onto one of my photos.

"Some of these people, for sure. And why? We don't need more religion in India. We have plenty religion", he said, rolling his eyes but also glancing towards his incense holder and the image of a deity on the bookshelf. "Is it just business? There are other ways to make money."

I saw my opportunity. This was an area in which I felt some confidence. I leaned forward in my seat eagerly, matching the passion in his voice.

"The missionaries are the forerunners of capitalism, Sir. They target the poor and the illiterate. They promise wealth and then come the jobs in factories - cheap labour for producing consumer goods for the West. Or for those who can read, call centres. I've written about it. It's in my portfolio, Sir. The missionaries are used to prepare the way for the spread of western imperialism and the further enrichment of the West."

I began to feel hopeful again. Mishra's head was nodding gently.

"And we need to prevent that from happening here," he said slowly. "I like your work, Banerjee, very much"

Oh, how my emotions rolled, but Roshan Mishra was no fool. He had not achieved his position through family connections, but sheer hard work and smart decisions. He was not about to take any risks for my sake.

"I'll be very happy to consider you for a permanent position."

It took a moment for the realisation to sink in, and the disappointment. I was still freelance with no assurance of income. I tried to think how to persuade him, how to react, but the acute disappointment and my desperation overwhelmed my senses as Mishra continued, easing himself back into his comfortable and large office chair.

"I suggest you locate yourself in the town of Baripada. There's opportunity, along the lines we've been talking about. A foreign missionary resides there...

I then made the second mistake of that interview, sailing back against the wind, interrupting him and confirming for Mishra that he had made the right decision.

"Sir, I came all this way, with my wife, on the basis of your letter." I even waved his letter at him.

"Oh, recently married?"

I was immediately on my guard. I nodded; he pretended passing interest, but it was more than that.

"She must be young."

I smiled, not committing either way.

"And beautiful, of course."

Again, I smiled. My senses were on high alert. I would not be drawn on the subject of my wife - Mishra did not need to know anything about her, even if it was only polite interest. He let it pass and returned to the subject of my employment.

"And as I said in my letter, we need someone of your calibre. But it'll be freelance for a few months at least."

"Freelance doesn't guarantee any income, Sir. I will not disappoint you. I came to Orissa for this position."

"And I need to justify your employment to my superiors. You are young. Inexperienced."

He was not just talking about me as a journalist. I controlled my disappointment, finally. Mishra seemed to relent, or perhaps he saw an opening.

"Listen to me. Baripada offers opportunity. We are planning to open an office there, just as soon as we can..." he paused, choosing his word, "acquire the right land to build on. That will mean possible promotion."

Now I was listening. He continued, lowering his voice for emphasis.

"The missionary I just mentioned - he's been there a long time. He's hard to pin down, that one. You bring me evidence of his illegal conversions and you will have your permanent position. I'll even loan you a decent camera."

He lifted that impressive looking camera, the one that now hung around my neck, from a drawer in his desk, holding it up like a trophy ready for the taking.

"Well?"

"If there's evidence, I'll find it, Sir."

"Then soon you'll be on permanent staff."

And so it was that we found ourselves on the bus to Baripada.

I was itching to start digging for dirt, to find the evidence that would secure me the coveted employment and make me a journalist whose articles leapt to the front page, but one has to eat and sleep and so does one's wife.

First we needed lodging and were fortunate to find a two- roomed, mud-brick home with a roof in need of new thatching, a remnant of a village that had been subsumed by Baripada's growth. The dusty path leading to the front door would be mud in the rainy season, and the roof would leak, but I planned to have moved well before then. All I needed was evidence of an illegal conversion; how hard could that be?

As it happened, I did not have to wait long to encounter the missionary who, I believed, was to provide the soil out of which my future would grow.

LEPERS

The market was teeming with people as we searched and bargained for essentials. I impressed upon Shanti the need to spend as little as possible. In her kindness, she didn't ask why. She just kept bargaining, which she was doing when I was distracted by a small gathering around a man, an Indian, who appeared to be preaching. I wandered over to listen and found myself a subject of his attention. I was carrying the only food we would be eating for a while: a large bag of rice. Unwittingly I provided an illustration for him.

"Christians are told to forgive their enemies," the man was saying, a statement that was met with some derision and humour from his listeners. He was not an elderly man, but was greying at the temples, so reasonably advanced in years. I wondered what financial benefits he received for this preaching, which I suspected he must be paid by the foreign missionary.

"Your reaction is right," he acknowledged. "How is this possible? Like this man here," (and this was where I became the subject) "we all have a burden. We have a burden of guilt and unforgiveness that we carry."

I did not like the attention, but far more annoying were the words, words that quickly cultivated anger in my breast. I was no longer a dependent school boy who had no right of reply. I wanted to shout him down. How dare he presume that I, or anyone else, had burdens of guilt or unforgiveness? How quickly I had forgotten my own feelings from the day before. But now all that was eclipsed by my noble cause.

"But when Jesus takes that guilt and unforgiveness, then we too can forgive others because we no longer have that burden weighing us down," he continued.

I would have argued, confident of my right and the anger mushrooming inside me, except for what happened next, turning anger to fear in an instant.

A boy, a beggar, no more than ten years of age, was wondering through the crowds, begging and no doubt seeking opportunities to steal. And Shanti, having completed her purchase and carrying the bag of vegetables, turned to join me. I suppose neither was looking where they were going in that moment. They collided. Shanti, conscious of the baby she was carrying, reacted to protect her stomach and called out instinctively, a cry that caused me to instinctively swing to her defence.

The boy, malnourished, but also aware of his secret, had leapt backwards and lost his footing. I moved swiftly toward them and aimed a vengeful kick at the wretch lying on the ground. Apparently he was familiar with such treatment and he expertly avoided contact. But in doing so his hand, a hand that had been holding his buttonless shirt closed around his neck, was needed to balance his deft avoidance. In that moment his shirt fell open.

Somebody screamed.

My second strike swung from its target in an avoidance manoeuvre of its own as I swivelled instantaneously towards Shanti, the bag of rice toppling in the swiftness of my act. I let it go, precious grains erupting from the bag as it split, rice flooding onto the dirt.

My only thought was Shanti. I shielded her from the crush as people put as much distance between themselves and the boy. Shanti had not seen what I had seen.

"The rice," she called.

"Leave it. Leper."

Yes, I knew there was a cure for leprosy, but it hadn't been around that long and the stigma of a curse such as this lingers for many decades in the psyche of a people. There is something at the edge of my memory that I still can't quite grasp - perhaps it is only a feeling

- but whatever it is, it causes me to baulk, even now, at the thought of leprosy. Times are changing, but back then, leprosy was still a curse in rural India. I think it is still so. Lepers are not readily accepted back in their communities, if at all.

The boy who had fallen and who was hopelessly trying to cover the appalling lumps and lesions on his shoulder and neck, was cursed with this sickness that above all others separates one from society, makes one an outcast, and an out-caste.

And we were closer than I wanted to be, on the edge of the wide circle that had formed around the boy, who was alone now on the dusty ground, staring despairingly at the crowd, they making the sign against evil, some shouting curses at him, others shouting at those pushing to see from the back of the crowd.

It happened in the middle of this chaos.

The clamour decreased, the crowd calmed, almost hypnotized it seemed, as a white man, a European in his fifties I guessed, stepped from the crowd. He stood looking at the boy for a moment - it seemed longer. Nobody spoke. He could not see the leprous lesions from the angle he had approached. He started forward.

Of course it crossed my mind that this was the missionary - Staines was his name. An Australian. Apparently he had been in Baripada for over 30 years. He wasn't the fly in, fly out variety. He was more dangerous. You didn't stick with something that long unless you had carved out a very comfortable life, filled with servants and luxuries you could not enjoy in your home country, or you were of the really hazardous variety: a fanatic.

Nevertheless, the man was walking right up to a leper, a boy cursed with a terrible, contagious disease, the treatment of which was and is difficult and time consuming. I scanned the crowd - they seemed spellbound, fascinated, watching.

Shanti felt as I did; we didn't know, and Mishra had not mentioned this aspect of Staines, the missionary.

'Do something, Baba,' she whispered.

I knew what she meant. I couldn't allow him, irrespective of who he was, to walk up to a leper unknowingly, even if everyone else was going to let him. It did make me wonder, fleetingly, if there was a suppressed animosity towards him amongst the people of this town.

I called out a warning, "Hey Mister, he's a leper."

He raised his hand in acknowledgement, but did not look my way, his eyes on the boy alone.

The boy turned at his approach, alerted by my call. His shirt fell open again and the full effect of the disease up his shoulder and across his chest was revealed. Shanti gasped. I quickly shielded her and tried to move her further away, but the crowd were not giving way at this climactic moment in the drama. I was angry with myself for not getting her away earlier. We were about to have a baby and proximity to a leper, looking at a leper, was asking for bad luck.

By this time Staines - yes, it was him, although I still wasn't certain at that point - had knelt down beside the boy and was talking to him. Then he did a thing that is still etched in my memory, something so foreign to my way of thinking that I could hardly grasp what my eyes were telling me. This man reached out both arms, took this boy in them and lifted him gently from the ground and held him close.

At that moment an experience from my youth on the streets of Kolkata flooded my memory in all its detailed and emotional clarity. We were walking on a busy street when my mother pulled me to the side, around a man lying in our way. He was moaning, trying to move, eyes glazed over from starvation and near death. My mother told me not to look, but it was a fascinating sight to a young boy. As I looked back at the man, I saw a small woman dressed in strange clothing kneel down next to him and begin to tend to him. Soon the sight was obscured by the throng of people, but the picture of humility kneeling next to pain, the depiction of compassion and hopelessness merging, that portrait was inexplicable, transcendent, 'other'. It was the only time I saw Mother Teresa.

The boy buried his head in the man's neck as he was carried

from the scene. Then the crowd parted, and quickly too, clearing a wide pathway for this impossible sight to depart along. Had I just witnessed a phenomenal display of courage, or was the man simply insane? I asked who the man was, already knowing the answer.

"That was Graham Staines."

Yes, that was my first encounter, and it left me in no doubt that Staines was a missionary of the hazardous variety: a true fanatic.

But I had a job to do.

I should have done more research, been more cautious, but I didn't have the luxury of time. How is one to know that misfortune lurks just beyond the next bend in the river, ready to throw one in?

My investigations into Christian activity in the area had quickly borne fruit... although that is too generous a description. I had seeds that could be planted, an encouraging start en route to the garden of delights that I was anticipating: a baptism by Christians of a young woman was to take place at a nearby village and a number of the villagers were anxious and annoyed. The primary reason for the baptism appeared to be the promised marriage of the girl to a Christian boy. Why not convert the other way around? It did not take much on my part to fuel the villagers discontent into a commitment to action. The plan was for a group of men to ambush the baptism and prevent it from happening. I, of course, would be present, together with my impressive camera, to capture the evidence.

I had to leave the house well before dawn to reach the place. After a long walk I made my way through the riverside reeds to find a suitable hide, a spot with a view of what I hoped was the location where the baptism would take place.

At the time, I remember, I was excited. I expected a successful disruption of the baptism, good photos with the telephoto lens and an excellent article to hand in to Mishra. If luck was on my side, I thought, Staines would not only be present, but also conduct the baptism. I still had a lot to learn.

That early morning was filled with anticipation for me. Even the mosquitoes could not suck it from me as I huddled at the water's edge, the steam gently resting just above the surface of the water, beautiful lilies, *kokaa*, a scattering of pink along the banks, opening up as if offerings on my part to the Goddess of Wealth.

It was not long before the tell-tale put-put of a motorbike approaching interrupted my dreams of Mishra's pleasure and my inevitable success. I remained hidden, practising patience. I had the right place; all I had to do was wait for the action.

The small group of Christians gathered at the waterside exactly where I had expected, but there was no sign of Staines -disappointing, but not ruinous to my expedition.

I waited, camera ready, for the moment of disruption as a local pastor took the young woman into the water, snatches of his words reaching me across the water.

"...The way, the truth..."

"...Do you believe..."

I could not hear her replies.

"...Of your own free will..." (I remember being struck by that line).

But it was happening too fast.

I risked raising my head above the reeds, scanning for the promised villagers.

"I baptise you in the name of the Father..."

And in she went, disappearing under the water, and still no sign of the disrupters. What was I to do? When next would I have such an opportunity?

Impulse urged me to action.

I intercepted their retreat to the road, determined to question the woman and challenge the proceedings, nullify them if I could. My anticipation of an easy success had heightened my disappointment, which in turn fueled my anger and determination to get something worthwhile out of this event.

The Christians quickly closed ranks around their prize who was now wrapped in a blanket against the cold, shrouded in her new cloak of protection and supposed righteousness, they hustled her away from my approach and the reality I represented. The pastor intercepted my inquiry, turning to block my advance and prevent me from getting anywhere close to the girl. He was smiling, pretending friendliness. He didn't just smile; he couldn't stop smiling - at his victory, I was sure.

I moved to get past him, calling, "What have you been promised?"

He bluntly blocked my path again, making it quite clear that he would physically prevent me from speaking to the girl, as if that insolent smile of his was compensation.

"Only what God promises, Sir."

He had the impudence to call me "Sir" while still standing in my way, no intention of treating me anything like a "Sir". I tried to push past him.

"I want to talk to *her*."

"You can talk to me, Sir."

"Where's your legal documents? Your affidavit?"

"Those are for the proper authorities, Sir, not for you."

It was the "Sir" again that really did it, and the superior attitude. I grabbed the wooden cross he had hanging around his neck.

"You think this gives you the right? Huh?"

With my other arm I shoved, really only trying to get past him...

I'm still not entirely sure how it happened. I suppose I pulled harder on the cross as a counterbalance to the push of my other arm. And he tripped as he stepped backwards, adding to the weight. Maybe I even tried to stop him falling - I don't know - but I do know that the thin leather around his neck snapped, and I know I was pulling hard at that moment, and I know that the bottom point of the cross with its metal cap smashed into my camera lens, badly cracking that expensive lens.

It sounds like a cliché to me now, but I honestly could not believe my bad luck. My first report, and I had not even taken a photo yet. I could not imagine what I was going to say to Mishra. I could see the certainty of a permanent position fading fast.

It took me a while to realise the pastor had hit his head on a rock when he fell. He was being assisted by a young man from the group, now shirtless as he wrapped it around the pastor's head to staunch the flow of blood. I vaguely heard "you may need stitches" as I tried to come to terms with my own tragedy; hardly a tragedy, but I was young and selfish, and that was how it seemed to me at the time. The first carefully cultivated opportunity for my garden of provision had been ravaged by a flash flood, the top soil carried away, leaving me with a few sick and straggly seedlings. In that moment I could not imagine how I was going to salvage the story, let alone rescue my reputation.

Ah, how experience of real tragedy changes perspective!

AN ASSIGNMENT

I had still not reached any solution in my head when I heard the motorbike start up. That galvanised me into action. I was not going to let the pastor get away with breaking the lens - it was he who stepped in front of me, more than once, refusing to let me do my reasonable and legal investigation.

I raced toward the sound, feeling deserted and enraged, determined to secure some recompense for the destruction they had caused to my property. They had dispersed quickly -efficiently I suppose, as I would not have known which path to follow to find the young woman now. But there was an elderly man with a bicycle still present.

What followed was like something out of a slapstick television comedy. If I had not been so desperate and distraught at the thought of not only losing all prospect of a job, but also having to pay for the lens with money I did not have, well...

I 'borrowed' the bicycle from the old man, promising to return it (which I did later), and proceeded to chase after the motorbike! How did I ever think I could catch a motorbike by the power of pedalling? I rode with the energy of anger, the camera and camera case bouncing on my back.

Foolish as my pursuit seems, they were actually travelling slowly, fearful that the pastor might faint and fall from the back of the bike. I still had them in sight at a point where the road they had taken made a wide curve around some fields. I took the short cut, going straight.

When I reached an irrigation ditch, without hesitation, I vaulted off and tried to leap over the ditch, carrying the bike. Of course, the weight of the bike limited my leap to about three quarters of the way across and I landed short, slipped and found myself face down in the mud.

I was determined, I'll give myself that. I jumped up, well, slithered actually, threw the bike out of the ditch, hauled myself into the next field and was on my way with not even a moment's reflection. Amazingly, when I reached the road again, I had in fact gained a little on my quarry.

But soon I was falling behind again. Then, rounding a bend, I met a herd of cows coming towards me, completely filling the road. The cows had, in fact, slowed the motorbike down and I saw my chance. With the bicycle held above my head, I pushed through the cows, nervously, as they were not liking the bicycle above their heads. But I made it through and energised by the ground I had gained I once again committed myself to the pedal.

Sweat was dripping off me and the mud was starting to dry in places when I saw the motorbike, much further ahead now, turn into a property that seemed to have a large gate-like structure. My head down I doubled my effort lest I lose sight of them now and did not look up again until I reached the property entrance.

Glancing up as I turned to follow them I was struck by horror. The gate did indeed have a large concrete arch above it, but it was a word across the metal gate that caught my eye. The word I saw was 'LEPROSY'.

Instinctively I hit the brakes, hard. The bicycle slid from underneath me and I ended up on my back, looking up at the sign: "MAYURBANJ LEPROSY HOME".

I was still staring at the sign when I heard a car horn sound behind me. The man in the car (I discovered later he was a doctor) was friendly enough.

"I need to go in."

He must have wondered about me - covered in mud and sweat, lying on the road. Coming to my senses I scrambled out of the way and retrieved the bicycle so that he could drive in through the gate. It was a gate I had no intention of entering, and the bitterness at having lost my quarry after such a chase galled me no end. But I was not going in.

And that was made all the more certain when I noticed a fingerless hand, just a fist without fingers, resting grotesquely on the gate itself. I followed with my eyes the scrawny limb attached to this stump, up to a thin face with vacant, watery eyes staring out from above half a nose. It was horrible. There was no way I was going in there. I had Shanti and the baby to consider.

What was I to do in my situation? Damage control is what it's called, I suppose, although I was not in control of much at that stage. I had to have something to show for the broken lens. I had to save my 'seedlings' and try to coax some life out of them. Despite my earlier despair I determined to turn the tragedy into triumph, and even convinced myself of success.

I wrote my article, exaggerating everything I could while Shanti washed my clothes and cleaned the camera - she found the pastor's cross in my pocket, but didn't tell me at the time as she didn't want to disturb me, knowing I was keen to take my article to Mishra that day. I wanted the pay. I wanted Mishra to see my quick work. I wanted praise for my interpretation of the facts.

And so I was soon back on a bus to see Mishra, eager despite the broken lens that I carried, believing that my brilliance outshone such trivialities; broken lenses were a small price to pay in the pursuit of real evidence.

I should have been less eager. Mishra was not pleased.

After a very long wait in the foyer, I eventually found myself in his office seated in the low chair, my eyes barely level with the ocean desk surface, as Mishra busied himself with his many responsibilities, saying things like 'you're the journalist; you're responsible,' I countering with things like 'one has to provoke a reaction at times to get the story,' all the while pretending calm to cover my increasing apprehension. Mishra seemed to have almost lost interest in me.

He said he would print the article 'somewhere' to help pay for the broken lens. My bravado in asking for an advance on my next piece was met with scorn.

"Your next piece?"

"I produce good material, Sir, even when nothing happened. You will not be disappointed."

"I feel like I've heard that somewhere before."

I was desperate to salvage something from the wreckage, determined not to back down. I'm not sure where this stand-off would have led if not for the interruption that then occurred, although as I look back now, I wonder if Mishra was not playing with me, setting me up for what was to come, manipulating me to a position where I might accept a certain proposal.

A large man, Raj was his name and, as I later learnt, a loyal chattel to Mr Mishra, entered the office and whispered something in Mishra's ear. The reaction was instantaneous and explosive, his face changing colour, eyes widening, spittle forming at the corners of his mouth as he spat words, staccato- like.

"Are you mad? I have no father! Get rid of him!"

This was not part of his plan, not part of his manipulation of me - the reaction was uncontrolled, the emotion too raw, too incredible, too exposed.

Raj left the room placidly; Mishra took a while to settle, mumbling to himself, but perhaps also for my benefit. He was not a man to readily show his true feelings.

"Mad people. My father is dead; dead a long time ago."

I felt discomfort at being witness to his distress and I honestly thought our meeting was over. I did not think Mishra would easily recover any magnanimity at that point, so it was with some surprise that I received the next exchange.

"I'm about to meet with some very important people."

"I'm sorry to keep you, Sir."

"Why don't you join me?"

If his intention was to throw me into confusion, he succeeded.

The meeting took place in the printing room, newsprint churning noisily through the machines around us. I was introduced to two gentlemen, apparently financially independent, possibly the owners of the newspaper, but none of this was divulged, not even their names, and I have never seen them since.

Mishra explained briefly that I was "hoping to expose the illegal activities of that missionary, Staines."

They obviously knew of 'that missionary, Staines,' because they actually took some interest in me then, one of them acting as spokesman.

"We applaud your purpose. Of course, you are not the first to try. Hard evidence is not that easily come by."

"If there is evidence I will find it, Sir."

They were not as easily convinced, and to be fair, I was 'young and inexperienced'; they were not. Thus we came to the real reason for inviting me to this meeting, although not all of their purposes were revealed to me at this time, nor ever.

"We are of the opinion that for success in this endeavour, someone, needs to become a 'Christian,' in order to gain their trust and thereby gather the necessary evidence."

The focus was on me - how would I react? Frankly, I thought it was somewhat extreme, but if they really wanted the evidence it was a reasonable plan, although I thought it could take quite a long time to achieve success, and I said so, politely.

"It would take no longer than all the unsuccessful attempts," was the gentleman's reply. "An endeavour worthy of support, don't you think, Roshan?"

Mishra agreed, and given his knowing that I was in need of money, I began to detect an inkling of a setup, although it was still far from the forefront of my mind at that stage. I knew I needed money and this was an opportunity I could not ignore.

And then came the deal breaker.

"Of course, the person doing this may have to enter into the service of lepers."

As I'm sure you can appreciate, something turned in my stomach, as it always did at the thought of leprosy and lepers. I tried to show curiosity; no doubt a stronger emotion showed in my face, my voice, my eyes as the gentleman continued.

"That is the veil behind which Staines operates. You may have to prove your conversion and loyalty."

I tried to remain nonchalant. I was beginning to think that this was the reason Mishra had not followed through on the offer he made in his letter, this was his preferred option, and this was what had kept his rage at the broken lens in check. I had to keep them thinking that I might accept this proposal.

"That would be something," I said. "I shall have to think about it."

"Of course. Well, I wish you success."

With that both gentlemen returned to their study of the broadsheet. The meeting was over. I turned to Mishra and Mishra turned to his assistant, Raj, who handed him a note. He glanced at it, then at me.

"It's for you. Your wife has gone into labour."

"But she's not due for a month."

"She's young."

He emphasised 'young'. I backed off, not sure if 'young' and 'early labour' were connected. I didn't want him prying there.

"I better go. Sir, about an advance..."

"I shall have to think about it," he said, matching my words exactly and making his point.

Going undercover, faking conversion and possibly even working to help lepers was the deal. They were convinced this was the way to go - no doubt they had experience of failure through more conventional methods. And they were not going to make it easy for me to say no. I needed money, I had a young wife and Mishra was clearly sniffing at the possible impropriety of this, and I had a child about to arrive, a child being born too early, at least a month too early. Of course, the child was the reason we were married. I confess to it now, but at the time I would do all in my power to prevent Mishra having access to that piece of information. Shanti had been pledged to marry someone else and her family, to put it politely, were unhappy with me.

The bus!

Lurching out of the depot like an angry elephant, I had to run to catch it, slapping its backside to get on board. The last bus of the evening... I wondered if Mishra had kept me waiting on purpose so that I would feel his irritation in having to stay the night.

The swaying elephant relented, slowing just enough for me to run alongside and leap up into the open door, a helping hand pulling me on board. Perhaps it would have been better if I had missed it.

I found a seat next to an elderly man and turned my thoughts to Shanti and the imminent arrival of the baby. I imagined her joy, not her loneliness; her excitement, not her fear; her anticipation, not her pain. In short, I had no concept of how much she needed me just then.

We had left the city and were well out in the open country before the 'elephant' turned on me with a vengeance.

I was still ignorantly enjoying my defective thoughts about childbirth when the conductor intruded. How had I not anticipated, thought about, prepared for this moment? I had left that morning with insufficient funds - intentionally. My plan was, if necessary, to empty my pockets in front of Mishra, showing him my reality, showing him that if he wanted articles he would need to do something. It was a bold plan. I had not anticipated Shanti going into labour. I had asked for an advance, why not a bus fare? At least Mishra may have given me that.

I knew, even before I reached into my inner jacket pocket, that I did not have enough on me to make up the fare.

I searched my pockets - the conductor had seen such displays before. I promised to pay the following day - the conductor was insulted that I should take him for such a fool. I pleaded that my wife had just gone into labour - the conductor was disbelieving and unmoved. I produced my journalist card, a sure sign of respectability - the conductor was unimpressed. I threatened to write a damaging story about his overcrowded bus, packing passengers in like cattle for slaughter - the conductor signalled for the driver to stop.

As the bus slowed and I prepared for a fight, the elderly man next to me leaned across to the conductor, the price of a ticket in his hand. The conductor was resolute; he had not taken kindly to my threats.

"Take it."

Reluctantly the money changed hands and the driver was signalled on his way. I was relieved and grateful.

"I'll pay you back."

"No need."

"No, I will pay you back."

"It was a gift to me. It's a gift to you."

I was grateful, of course, but I reflected little on the implications of such generosity at the time. I believed in karma of course, and generosity is rewarded, yet I was not an obvious recipient. I was not a beggar, I was not a holy *sadhu*; I was healthy, well-dressed and apparently educated. The reward for generosity to such as I was doubtful at best.

My thoughts, however, were not on such philosophical perplexities; they were firmly fixed on my immediate circumstances as the adrenalin eased, my body experiencing the aftershocks of an avoided battle.

I reached for the old man's water bottle.

"May I?"

He hesitated. Strange for a man who had just paid my bus fare, I thought.

"Not if it's a problem."

"No, no, it's fine," he responded hurriedly, and passed the bottle.

"All Indians are brothers, ne?" I smiled, quoting the Pledge before I lifted the bottle and drank.

I drank.

I drank from that bottle.

Even now, even after all I've been through, this I still would not do.

As I drank, two children sitting on the floor of the bus picked up on the words of the Pledge.

"India is my country and all Indians are my brothers and sisters."

As I returned the bottle to the old man I noticed his fingers for the first time. As they curled around the bottle I handed him, right there next to mine, I saw the damage, the ends missing.

I knew!

Although I was not listening, the children continued their recitation: "I love my country and I am proud of its rich and varied heritage. I shall always strive to be worthy of it."

My eyes travelled up his arm to his neck where the collared shirt didn't quite cover the skin discolouration caused by leprosy medication.

"I shall give my parents, teachers and all elders, respect, and treat everyone with courtesy..."

Even his nose was slightly damaged where the leprosy had eaten away the flesh. Easy to see now that I knew.

I rose from my seat. I knew I was going to vomit.

The old man - Sundar! His name was Sundar, as I later discovered - instinctively stretched out that grotesque claw of his, trying to calm me. Anything but!

My movement had drawn attention. His sleeve fell back enough on his outstretched arm to reveal more of his ghastly secret.

I think it was the mother of the children who started screaming. I was already heading for the door.

The elephant slid unceremoniously to an abrupt halt in the gravel and disgorged passengers, of which I was the first. I fell to my knees and similarly disgorged the contents of my stomach.

I must have remained there for a while, staring out into the dusk, feeling wretched and bewildered at this turn of events. How much bad luck can come one's way in a single day?

One should not tempt the gods with such questions.

The roar of the now wrathful elephant alerted me as it plunged back into its journey, pitching and swaying over the road shoulder. The shock of disbelief cost me a few seconds, then I was on my feet, racing after that ancient beast, yet again slapping its backside.

But this time the beast only glared back at me, its red eyes reducing as it fled into the gloom, revenge complete.

I stood in the middle of the road, in the middle of the most remote stretch of that road, in the middle of a maddening mix of emotions consuming me.

I wanted to hurl that bus from the road and repeatedly smash it into the great rocks growing out of the landscape. I wanted to rip that driver and that conductor limb from limb. I wanted to assuage my rage on someone.

Interestingly I didn't feel that way about the old man now standing forlorn, further back on the road, now only a smudge in the fading light. Perhaps it was fear, or perhaps a camouflaged sympathy for a fellow human being whose karma had fallen fiercely on his life; whatever it was, I had no wish to wreak vengeance on this fellow-sufferer, even if he was the apparent cause of my misfortune. I just wanted to get away from him. So I turned and started on the long walk to Baripada.

The few vehicles still travelling a lonely road in the night are wise not to stop for fear of bandits. A moment of compassion could cost their belongings, their vehicle, or even their life.

I waved when lights approached.

I watched when they passed.

I walked on when they were gone.

A BABY

It was some hours later and the cold was gnawing through my clothes when I heard the approach of another vehicle. I didn't even bother to turn around this time, just kept walking, concentrating on a rhythmic pace aimed at keeping the cold out without exhausting the body's reserves.

But the vehicle, a Jeep of sorts, had no sooner passed when it braked and came to a standstill not far ahead of me. I stopped. My first instinct was caution. What if these were bandits seeking easy prey? My luck was not to be trusted - the day had taught me that well enough.

But what could they take? My clothes? I had no money. And what of Shanti? I had to think of her.

The front passenger door opened and a figure stepped out, climbing then into the back seat, leaving the front door open. For me. It was a chance I had to take.

The decision made I was suddenly very keen to be in the warm vehicle on my way to Shanti's side. You can imagine my shock when, in the dim light of the cab, the face of Graham Staines confronted me. My greeting literally died on my lips. He spoke in Oriya, not English, apparently amused by my frozen expression.

"*Namaskaar. I won't bite.*"

I retrieved my voice from somewhere. "My wife is having a baby." I mean, why else would one be out on a lonely road in the middle of the night? I was a journalist. I was supposed to be good with words. But he didn't mock or laugh, just smiled.

"Well, let's get you home."

I climbed into the passenger seat, cursing my stupidity. This was the man I was to investigate. It was not the introduction I had hoped for, nor did I want to be in his debt.

I turned to greet the passengers in the back seat - a man and a woman - as the vehicle bounced back onto the bitumen. And stared into the eyes of Sundar, the leper from the bus.

"Leper. He's a leper," I spluttered.

Staines' reply was calm.

"Was. He's been cured for years."

It was all too much for me. The coincidence, the fear, the suspicion, the doubt.

"Stop the car."

"Relax. You..."

"Stop the car!"

"Okay, okay. Calm down.

He began to pull over, applying the brake. It was another comedy moment like the whole bicycle incident - the country air seemed to have sucked composure and dignity from me. I was in a hurry. I stepped out before the vehicle had fully come to a halt and plunged into the dust and darkness next to the road.

Staines jumped out of the vehicle, sensibly waiting until it had come to a complete standstill, and came looking for me, apparently concerned for my welfare. But I was now convinced something was going on. Covered in dust and embarrassment, but with no other damage, I went on the attack.

"What are you doing?"

"Offering you a lift."

"Is this a setup? Huh? He pays for my ticket, the bus leaves, you turn up..."

You have to admit, from my perspective it did look too much of a coincidence. I didn't know that Sundar lived at the Leprosy Home and Staines had come to fetch him because the woman in the car, the other passenger, had reported the bus incident to him. She had been on the bus, but I didn't know that. Admittedly, Staines tried to explain all that, but I was not able to hear at that point.

To me it looked like a setup.

Staines was not unkind, I suppose, but he was not about to enter a debate.

"Do you want a lift?"

"Not with a leper."

"He's not a leper. He was cured 30 years ago."

"It's him or me."

"Well then it's him. I'll give you a moment to think about it."

With that, he walked back to his vehicle and climbed into the driver's seat. I stayed where I was.

He called out one more time, "You said your wife's having a baby. Are you sure you don't want a lift?" before my last chance of a lift left me to the night, the two evil red eyes of the vehicle diminishing in the darkness.

As Shanti wasn't due for a month, I convinced myself that it was a false alarm, that there was no real urgency, that I did not need to be home.

Becoming a parent evokes new instincts and feelings; at least it did so for me. Even now, all these years later, despite the impositions and burdens of parenthood, I experience an overwhelming instinct to protect. Back then I was only vaguely aware of this, but I did have similar feelings towards Shanti, who had given up all her security to be with me. I had to protect her, and bringing the curse of leprosy into our home was not something I was prepared to risk. A night in the cold and a long walk was a small price to pay.

If only I had known, so many things, I would have made a different decision that night.

I walked. I found some shelter and slept poorly for a few hours. I walked some more.

In the morning I found a temple and took advice on how to cleanse myself before returning home. I shivered uncontrollably in the river water, performing the ritual bath and muttering the prescribed prayers.

I was probably feeling sorry for myself as I approached our small abode. The *Hijra* (eunuchs) alerted me. They began to dance at my approach, guessing that I was the father. I ran past them, throwing open the door, the guilt at my absence already burdening me.

A wizened old midwife was holding a baby - my baby. Shanti's baby. Our baby. I felt out of control, unsure of what to do.

"Shanti?"

"She sleeping, Sir," said the old woman. "Sorry, you have a daughter."

I wasn't sorry. Sons are heavily favoured in India; daughters cost money in dowries and the like. But I wasn't sorry. I was relieved. I remember looking at that strange little face, so small, so foreign, so ugly - I know women cannot think of babies as ugly, but the toothless face of the newborn is seldom in proper proportion, the skin sits loose on the frame and has the look of something that has been bottled in liquid too long. Although this one was conforming to 'normality' - enough time had passed in air.

The midwife tried to hand the baby - our baby - to me to hold, but I wasn't quite ready. She looked as if I might break her. I used the dancing and ululating of the *Hijra* as my excuse and retrieved some cash from a pot - one of our hiding spots. It is believed that the *Hijra* can bless or curse a baby, so it is wise to pay them, just in case. I had risked curses enough in my encounters with leprosy.

I joined the *Hijra* for a dance, holding off on paying until the mood was bright. Dancing about is not exactly my favourite pastime - I'm too serious. Nevertheless, it was not too difficult. After my unpleasant night, then the guilt at realising Shanti had indeed been in labour, I felt such relief at the birth having gone well that I was perfectly happy to dance. I distributed notes in the process of the dance, too few to delight them, but sufficient to placate them. Given the opulence of our dwelling they did not expect too much.

My return to the house brought about the first shock to my already exhausted emotional state.

The baby - our baby - was now sleeping in a box on the table and there, lying with our baby, in the box with our baby, right there next to her head, was something incomprehensible to me. It was as if the gods were toying with me, laughing at me. There before me lay a symbol of all I had been fighting to avoid, a reminder of my defeats and frustrations: a curse.

I over-reacted, of course, but I was tired and fragile after all I had been through.

The wooden cross, the very same cross that had hung on the neck of that belligerent preacher, the very same that had smashed my camera lens, the very same that represented and sided with the lepers who had prevented me from being here for Shanti in her hours of need, that cross, somehow forgotten in my pocket when I had returned from that useless baptism, that cross, albeit with teeth marks in it now - apparently the midwife had thought it a suitable item for Shanti to bite down on in her pain - that cross was now lying with my daughter, mocking me, reminding me, cursing me.

I was cold with anger.

"What is this?"

"Sorry, Sir. She need something to bite, Sir. For the pain."

"I don't want this in my house!"

I woke the baby... so much for 'sleeping like a baby'.

"I found it in room, Sir."

I couldn't exactly blame the midwife, could I? I stalked out of the house, giving the *Hijra* a moment's hope, but only a moment before I hurled the accursed object into bushes alongside the road, as far away as I could.

I needed my wife. I needed Shanti's calm, her steadying influence, her confidence in me.

Of course my antics had woken her as well, so I was at last able to see her. Her look of tenderness, admiration, love... it never failed to still my struggling soul.

She looked exhausted. But she was so pleased to see me. No reproach, no admonition, just gratefulness. As I knelt down next to her she raised her hand to my cheek. She didn't even ask what the shouting was about.

"It's nothing. I've dealt with it now," I said anyway.

"She's beautiful, ne?"

"Yes. Like you."

She smiled weakly and closed her eyes. I was back and all was well in her world again. How was it possible that I seemed to be all she needed? I, on the other hand, still needed to deal with my guilt.

"I should have been here."

"You're here now."

I left her to sleep then, yet again struck by the phenomenal serenity she seemed to possess. It was a serenity I needed, especially in what happened next.

I was still marvelling at this wonderful woman who was my wife when the midwife intruded.

"One thing, Sir."

I was happy to pay her fee, even though we were short on cash.

"That not it, Sir."

I went cold again, not with anger this time, but with fear.

"The baby...?"

"She very well. Everything fine."

I sighed, smiling - my recent poor luck was making me paranoid.

"It your wife."

I could not breathe. I could not speak.

The midwife held a handful of cloths. She opened them for me to see - blood. For a moment I thought, "That's normal, right?" But then she clarified.

"I have done all. Still she bleeds."

I stared at her, trying to comprehend what she was really saying. Then she made clear the seriousness of what she was saying.

"Maybe they help at hospital."

I don't really remember much of what happened next. I suppose the mind or heart sort of shuts down at so much emotional assault. I did what I had to do, mechanically.

I think I lost hope. I was certainly completely overwhelmed by a sense of helplessness. My belief in my ability to have a measure of control over my circumstances was utterly shattered. When a large tree is uprooted, how can it grow again?

Apparently I got Shanti onto a bullock cart, the slowest form of transport! But gentle also, I suppose.

I do remember walking next to the cart. I remember anger returning to accompany me as I walked. At first it was at the slowness of the cart - worthless anger - bullocks walk; that's what they do.

Slowly the anger transferred, turning on the gods who seemed to be playing with me, callously tossing me from side to side. But deities are not tangible and though I was wary of them, paying them due respect, I preferred to trust in my own efforts rather than endless supplications and petitions. Old habits die hard. That self-reliant tree, even lying on its side and dying, was all I had.

Finally the anger came to rest, a low brooding anger, settling on the leper who had prevented me from getting home in time, on the Christian who had chosen to give him a lift instead of me, and on the other Christian who had soured my first assignment with a broken camera lens.

I remember hopelessly counting out the last of my meagre cash supply to an indifferent admissions clerk at the hospital. I remember my shock at seeing Shanti hooked up to a drip, a doctor and nurse working around her. I remember the doctor handing me a list of purchases that I could not afford. I remember noticing that this was the same man who had driven into the grounds of the Leprosy Home when I had been lying in the gateway, covered in mud.

I remember... I remember it was my anger that moved me to action.

RELATIVES AND MONEY

Yes, I think it fair to say that without my anger I would not have taken that next step. Although I was not aware of it at that stage. It was a low thing, under the surface of conscious thought.

I needed money and could think of only three avenues, all of which filled me with dread. The third was impossible - indentured labour for the child - she was too young. In the city a child this young might be sold, but not in the rural setting. And how would Shanti have felt about that? Perhaps I romanticize her, but I think Shanti would rather have given her life than do that to her child.

The first avenue was unpleasant, but not impossible. Of course, it represented great cost to myself; I realized even in my dazed state that it could be the end of my marriage. I was the hated thief who had stolen an imperious man's favourite daughter. I had not been well received; I did not expect a pleasant reception now. But Shanti had a chance.

Near the hospital were some small shops providing services to the unfortunates who found themselves or their relatives in hospital. One had a telephone service. The mobile network one finds in the cities now did not exist in 1999.

I dialled the number.

Do you know the feeling? It's physical. The weight that sinks into one when the required action can only bring a form of tragedy, when the situation is such that the necessary act must bring pain, be it grovelling humility or abject rejection, when the mind's desperate hope seems to descend into the body itself under a smothering mass of despair and dread.

The phone was answered with a simple 'hello' - I did not recognise the voice.

"Namaskaar. It's Manav Banerjee. I..."

The phone went dead.

I waited. I gathered strength again.

I dialled.

"Please don't hang up. It's Shanti. She's in hospital..."

The phone was already dead.

The third time I dialled the phone had been unplugged.

I had to return to our little house to find more telephone numbers and chose that of a favourite aunt. Surely here I would find sympathy. When she answered the call I was quick.

"I'm calling about Shanti. Shanti's unwell; she's in hospital."

No reply, so I kept going.

"She needs help."

There was a long pause. I could feel the aunt struggling on the other end of the line and hope emerged again. I pressed my advantage.

"Can you help her?"

"I... I don't know anyone of that name."

"Please... please, I'll..."

"Goodbye."

I just sat for a while, that dead weight of despair sinking deeper within me.

How could they be so callous?

But her father was... how shall I put it? Very clear in what he believed. He was also the authoritarian head of the extended family. And he felt that Shanti had betrayed him, betrayed and dishonoured the family, and rejected all that had been given and promised to her. So he rejected her in return.

I didn't mention it earlier, but this was one of the main reasons we were willing to take work in a remote location. I honestly believe my life may have been in danger - once I was nearly beaten up by a couple of thugs. I cannot say for sure that they had been sent to deal with me, but there seemed no other reason; they didn't try to rob me, just beat me. Fortunately I can run fast. I got away before they could do too much damage.

So I wasn't dead, but as far as Shanti's family was concerned, we may as well have been. We were receiving the just reward for our sin.

I should mention that with my parents both deceased, I had spent the little that was left to me on my final years of education. I had relatives, of course, but no siblings. My mother remarried after my father's death and I never saw those relatives again. The man she married was not kindly toward me and a good education at a boarding school was his gift, to himself more than to me - it got me out of the house. I was glad to be gone.

But that was the past and it had little bearing on the present. Certainly I could see no avenue of assistance there.

So I sat in disbelief, desperate, dazed and wondering how I, and Shanti, could possibly deserve such bad luck. We loved each other - that was all! Why was that such a dreadful sin? I could not believe it, or was not prepared to believe it.

I don't claim to understand suffering. I can see other possibilities, other interpretations for it now. Back then I only felt the injustice of it; my experience offered only one interpretation. So I did, subconsciously, what most of us do: I looked for someone else to blame.

Thus it was my anger at Staines and his lepers that really moved me to make my next call. But I had nowhere else to go. This was the second and only other option I could envisage. I hoisted my fragile sail and set my course for Roshan Mishra.

I tried again for an advance, but Mishra was not a charity.

"My wife is in hospital."

"That's a family issue," he said simply, and I wondered again if he knew more than he had let on. But I could not ponder those possibilities then. It was time to take the next step.

"What if I become a Christian?"

There was a pause, then his voice, clearer, louder, interested - I think he was on speaker phone before, but had now lifted the receiver.

"Convert?" he asked.

"Yes."

He clarified the terms - everyone had to be convinced it was a genuine conversion, the purpose was to expose fraudulent conversions, and if this meant treating lepers I had to be prepared to do it...

What choice did I have?

And Mishra was true to his word - even generous. He arrived later that day: the hospital was paid, I was given an envelope full of cash - my retainer - and the use of a scooter that Raj brought up. It was more than I expected. And it indebted me to Mishra. I was grateful. The matter of the reneged promise of employment lay forgotten.

To this day I'm not sure if this was what Mishra had hoped for all along, or if it was merely circumstantial. Not that it matters now.

Shanti was receiving the best treatment a small-town doctor and hospital can provide, and that was all that mattered for that moment.

And now my optimism re-asserted itself.

Evidence. Evidence was everything. With evidence, no conversion was needed. The flood waters had abated and evidence was what would hold further flooding at bay.

I didn't know I was in a desert. I didn't recognise that the waters of my so-called 'flood' were indeed, evidence. Just not the sort of evidence I was looking for. And the plants I was trying to cultivate were desert plants. There are plants that are cultivated in deserts, but often with water from deep under the ground.

Enough talk of plants and metaphors and trying to make sense of it all.

"Follow the lead you have" and what I had was an illegal conversion. At least, I had an article about an illegal conversion. It appeared at the bottom of the front page - better than 'somewhere' - with a photo to prove the baptism took place! Of course, it was not a photo of the actual event. I had not taken any photos. But that is inconsequential - the baptism had indeed taken place.

It was a most satisfying moment in what were otherwise highly distressing circumstances, that moment of finally picking up the paper, flipping through it in search of the article, disappointment, then back to the front page... and there it was! Relief and joy - no, not quite, but victory, if victory can be a feeling. It gave me a way forward. It gave me hope.

I slapped the paper down on the desk in front of an officer at the Police Station.

"Fill out an FIR," I demanded.

He took his time to read the article, or make as if he was reading it. An FIR is a 'First Information Report' that kick-starts criminal proceedings.

Thinking about it now it was not only arrogant of me, it was foolish. If I really wanted to trap Staines, the last thing I needed was to alert him further by bringing the police into the investigation. But I wanted an easy way out. If I could link him to an illegal conversion, surely that was all it would take. Ah, the optimism of youth.

The officer was older, more experienced and more cynical than I. Which means he was unimpressed.

"No point."

"Money changed hands."

"Yes, every time you buy something."

"Buying and selling religion is against the law."

When I politely started quoting the relevant law to him, he saw that I was not going to be easily put off. Some action was required.

I was disappointed that the first point of contact was the perpetrator, not the victim. The officer called the pastor, asking him to meet at the convert's village. I suggested this was unwise, that the pastor might warn the girl, arrange a cover up... I was becoming annoying.

"How do you think he will reach the village before me? Unless you want to keep talking. I can listen to you and he can go to the village first."

That shut me up.

We found the girl at her place of work, threshing rice for a village land-owner. The lady who managed the workers, the wife of the land-owner, was unimpressed by the interruption, less impressed with the reason for it, and even more unimpressed by the argument put forward by the pastor:

"One day off a week is reasonable. She wants to come to church."

"During rice harvest!?"

Unintimidated, she kept right on at him, expressing the religious conflict that had arisen, "How would you know? You don't offer puja, you till the land during..."

"But we pray for you."

"To be converted, yes," I quipped.

Then the lady articulated the practical argument, "If I give her a day, the others will also want. Then they take two days, three days..."

She was rightly expressing the conflict that such traditions had. A day off each week did not match the needs of the agricultural lifestyles in the villages, organised as they were around a seasonal cycle: a time for preparation and tilling followed by rest as the crops grow, a time for harvest, threshing and storage, followed by rest in the fallow season.

The church tradition seems to have developed in conflict with such agricultural environments.

We were interrupted by the return of the girl in question, carrying the small package she was given at the baptism.

Of course, there was no money in the package and she denied ever receiving any. The package contained an Oriya New Testament of the Christian Bible.

I made a feeble argument, showing the officer where she had been 'forced' to sign the book:

"See, forced to sign."

"That's ownership," the pastor responded.

"No, that's conversion."

The officer had seen and heard enough. The pastor promised to do the legal paperwork for conversion and he was on his way.

"Is that it?" I called after him as the lady harangued her workers behind me, reminding them to "come to work" and not to "take liberties".

The officer was enjoying himself, I think.

"I could arrest you for assault," he responded, referring to the cut on the pastor's head.

"He broke my camera."

"Fill out an FIR."

It was a good retort, I see that now - my opening words thrown back in my face. At the time, of course, I was furious, not so much by the retort, but by feelings of hopelessness and fear and frustration.

"Follow the lead you have" is of no good when it leads to no thing you can use.

I was back at the hospital when I faced up to the reality of my next "lead".

Shanti was stable and that made it possible to think. And listen.

It was a radio news broadcast that moved me this time. I was resting against a wall, feeling sorry for myself. The sounds of the surrounds were sashaying unobtrusively around me when the broadcast ambled over:

"'Missionaries do not belong here', he said, throwing his weight behind the 'Quit India' movement. The General Secretary was addressing a rally in Maharashtra. He cited recent violence against Christians as justified reactions to forced conversions."

I was not alone. It was time the missionaries quit India and I was going to be part of that process.

It was time to step up and step out. It was time to go to the source. It was time to go to Staines.

I would like to tell you I confidently planned my next move. I would like to tell you this new clarity gave me clarity of action. I would like to, but it was not the case.

I was terrified.

Too strong a word? Perhaps, but there was so much depending on this: the job, Shanti, the child, the future, journalism... failure.

Where could I go if nothing was uncovered? There would be no other avenue, except the one. Conversion.

No doubt for some this is a small thing, a vagary of life necessary for survival or success, an expediency, even an opportunity. After all, wasn't this what many of the so-called conversions were? Mere convenience?

Why not me?

Indeed, why not me?

Even now, I still don't fully understand my objection. Was I so imbued with integrity? No, I can claim no such saintly quality. There was the threat of leprosy, of course, but it was more than that. An obstinacy, an unbendingness anchored me to 'my way'. It was evident in much of my doings. I had learnt to 'make do' independent of others, and I did not bow with ease to the will of others. Conversion was not my idea - it was being forced upon me.

I resented that.

And I feared it.

STAINES

A stake-out. That's what was needed. Not so much to stake out the terrain I was about to enter, nor to see something happen that was illegal, but to stake out my own mind and emotions to clarify how I was going to proceed.

Of course, in the process of staking out my mind and heart, I rode my scooter to the Mission Compound, to the Leprosy Home, to wherever Staines was traveling. I watched. I waited. I wrote my notes.

I followed him. I saw money change hands. I saw lepers being paid. But it was not that simple. He paid them for sabai grass mats and ropes which he delivered to the markets - nobody would have bought them if they had known the original source.

I saw meetings of Christians in surrounding villages. I saw food delivered - to Staines. In exchange for books and teaching materials. I saw him visit a hostel for girls, girls who came from remote villages, girls who otherwise would never have an education.

Evidence?

Nothing.

I saw him return a cured leprosy patient to her home. That caused some interest. Apparently the husband was expecting her but nobody else in the village was pleased to have a leper back and drawing water from the communal well. They were convinced the curse would spread and were far from convinced she was cured.

Shortly after Staines and his wife left, I interviewed the couple in their home. They were nervous and guarded. Rightly so. At first I thought it because Staines had sworn them to secrecy, or paid them, or forced conversion, or perhaps the woman had been returned to her home for refusing to convert. It turned out none of these were true.

It hadn't taken long for word to spread in the village and while I was still with them stones clattered onto the tiled roof of their humble dwelling. Some village children had been quick to take up the offence their parents felt at the leper's return, taking the opportunity to feel childish excitement at the presence of danger.

Here at least was a possible story, but not something that would draw me any closer to my goal. I was avoiding the inevitable. My hapless little boat could not stay in the bay any longer. I had to sail out into the broad unknown, beyond the horizon and away from that which was safe.

I finally realised that I already had an angle, a way of approaching Staines, when reading over my notes. Each path of investigation led to either a dead end, or, and this was the clincher, to some good that Staines was doing.

All I needed to do was write a story about the man who walked into that market place and picked up a small boy with leprosy. Who can resist a heart-warming story of bravery, compassion and self-sacrifice? At least, I felt sure, Staines would be happy to have a story about the good he was doing. But I didn't yet know the man.

I squared my sail and set forth with a smile installed, ready for use.

The entrance to the Mission Compound is crowded with shops on a busy street. Then one steps into another world - a large open area, a distinct divergence from the turbulence to the calm, although I was not feeling calm. A church building is set in the left corner of the open compound; a little further on, the mission house. Beyond that are some smaller buildings. Large trees provide shade and there is enough room for a healthy game of cricket, a game in which children were engaged when I entered the grounds, an upright car tire their makeshift wicket.

The Staines boys, Philip and Timothy, with their blonde hair and fair skin, stood out amongst their playmates. I was interested to see a couple of girls playing with them - not something one saw often.

I was distracted by the game as I approached the house where two vehicles were apparently being loaded, so it was with some shock that I discovered Staines closer than expected, already talking to me, anticipating and countering what I might be there for - and he was right.

"Ah, it's the man who chose to walk," was his opening, recognising me as the recalcitrant who had refused his charity. "Must have been a long walk."

"Yes...", I started, expecting the opportunity to introduce myself and state the reason for my presence. But Staines sailed past these expectations without any difficulty.

"How's your wife?"

"Oh, fine. She's fine."

"Great. And the baby?"

"Also fine."

"Boy or girl?"

"Girl."

"Congratulations. My first was a girl. Wonderful blessing."

The man kept talking! It was not what I had planned. But he had remembered that my wife was having a baby and seemed concerned and caring and... well, the wind had changed course; my sail, or tongue, was flapping. Staines, on the other hand, was sailing before a benevolent breeze.

Finally, he gave me a chance, of sorts.

"I'm sorry I couldn't give you a lift. So, what can I do for you?"

"Oh, I'm a journalist, and...

"Yep. I know."

"Yes, and I was amazed and shocked when you walked into that crowd in the market place and picked up that boy, physically..."

"That was nothing."

"No, but it was...'

"Mate, he's just a sick kid. No big deal. What's your name?"

"Manav Banerjee."

Why was he asking all the questions?

"Nice to meet you properly. I'm Graham Staines."

He was in control. I was the amateur.

"Write stories about people who really suffer in this society - the lepers, like that boy. Not me."

"I know I didn't want the lift, but I'm still impressed with the work you do."

"Then write about the work. Not about me."

"But it's your work."

"We'll talk about it when I get back. I've got a jungle camp to go to."

And with that, I was dismissed. But I had finally trimmed my sail and found some wind.

"A gathering of Christians in a village?" I confirmed.

He stopped, for just a moment, before continuing and telling me more than I'd asked. An invitation? A challenge?

"Yep. We're going to Monoharpur. Other side the mountains, then off through the foothills. Remote, but there's a scattering of Christians in the surrounding villages and a small church there. We do what we can to help them. I've got to pack. I'll speak to you when we get back."

I was not going to be that easily dismissed. I was sailing into the wind, but that was expected and I could tack, back and forth, as needed.

I returned to watching the cricket. Timothy was only six years old, but already had impressive control of both bat and ball. Australians were annoyingly good at cricket.

I drifted towards the gate very slowly, making myself as unobtrusive as possible, watching the cricket, observing the packing of water, supplies, bedding... attentive to actions and interactions.

My patience paid off.

I spotted the woman from the village, the woman Staines had returned to her husband only the day before, the woman apparently cured of her leprosy, the curse the villagers did not want back in their midst, that woman, Champa by name, I spotted her talking to Staines.

Well, begging or pleading are better terms. I moved closer on a different trajectory, able to get close enough to hear some of the exchange with a vehicle between us, feigning interest in the contents being packed.

I didn't understand all of it - mostly spoken in a local dialect in which Staines was apparently fluent. I learnt later he was conversant in at least two of the local dialects, as well as Oriya. What was clear, however, was that the woman was distraught, imploring help.

I was surprised.

Staines remained unmoved.

He turned to one of the mission workers.

"Give her a meal. She may not stay."

He left the sobbing woman to be escorted away with her grief intact and returned to the vehicle. To me, to be exact. Staines had not missed the fact that I was still about and had not missed the fact that I was eavesdropping.

"You think I'm harsh?" he asked.

I didn't answer, acting as if it was none of my business.

"She brought alcohol into the Home. I can smell it on her now. Alcohol lowers the effectiveness of the medication. I can't allow it."

"The village is not happy," I murmured.

"It's time they caught up. She's no longer contagious. She just has to keep up with her medication."

"So you won't help her anymore?"

Some of his frustration, or fear at what I might write, was seeping through.

"I am helping her!"

Was he trying to convince himself as much as me?

"Getting her back home to her village as soon as possible is the best thing I can do for her."

It then became clear that Staines was well aware of the danger I presented as a journalist. He had been aware from the very start and far from wanting publicity, he was seeking ways to avoid it.

He spotted the old man, the old man with whom I had refused to travel, the old leper who had shared his putrid water with me, the sight of whom was a nauseating reminder of my predicament. Staines leapt on the opportunity to direct me away from himself.

"You want a story, right? There's a story. Sundar. He's not had leprosy for 30 years, yet an educated man like you did not want to travel in the same vehicle as him."

I mumbled something about karma, my baby, my wife... which was true for me, but I suppose makes little sense in the scientific context and the 30 year time span.

Staines was quickly dismissive.

"He's suffered enough for his karma. He's actually dead, you know? They performed the death ceremony in his village. Another reason to get people home sooner rather than later."

Of course, times have changed, however slowly, and even though lepers are not welcome back in a village, they are unlikely to be officially declared dead. Back then it was different. Once the ceremony was performed, any sightings of the dead person was considered to be terrible bad luck, and not the person of course, but the manifestation of an evil spirit using the person's likeness to thereby bring evil upon those who foolishly acknowledged the apparition.

If Sundar had been declared dead, then to his village, his family, his loved ones, he was dead. And any interaction with him would be more than avoided; it would be hateful and horrifying. Utter rejection.

As for me, I had no desire to pursue a story about stomach-turning Sundar. Even so, I could see that those noble gentlemen who had placed me on this path knew more than I. To convert would be to work with lepers - I wasn't even close and already I was being asked to write about them, write their intimate stories. I wasn't ready.

"I don't think our readers..." I began, feebly seeking alternatives.

Staines simply ignored me.

"Can you imagine being treated as if you were dead, for years and years?"

"Readers are interested in what's happening now, and what you did..."

"For him, it's still happening now. When he was healed, I took him back to his village. His own son fled into the forest from him, terrified. He knew what had happened. I thought it was just the leprosy. All we had to do was explain that he'd been healed. But he knew. He kept calling out, 'I'm not dead'. Over and over. 'I'm not dead. I'm not dead.'"

Staines was lost in the memory for a moment. Either it was a real experience or he was a brilliant actor.

Then he turned back to me, smiling again, friendly. Apparently.

"Come talk to him and check out the Leprosy Home. I'll take you around when I get back."

Dismissed again. I tacked again.

As he called his sons from their cricket game, I pushed a little further, asking what it was that motivated him.

"Hey, I said no articles about me."

"Do you hope the lepers will become Christians?"

He was forthright.

"Of course."

"Why?"

"Because Jesus gives life, real life. But if you want the real story, you have to follow the Lord Jesus."

And there it was.

Staines the missionary. The purpose of all he did was to convert. Oh, to trap him in it! Telling me to follow the story of Jesus was not nearly enough. But we were making progress. Navigation points were emerging.

What could I have asked or said? What would have been the perfect next line? I certainly could not have seemed too keen on the idea, nor did I want to dismiss it outright. Run before the sudden squall or pull back on the rudder...

As it was, no decision was needed. The squall passed as suddenly as it appeared, replaced by a dead calm.

A voice from behind me said, "This is the man, Graham."

The pastor, as I viewed it, who broke my camera. I had wasted no time making enemies.

"He's looking for evidence," the pastor continued.

Staines was looking right at me when he replied calmly.

"I know. He has a right to look."

Clearly, I wasn't fooling Graham Staines. Yet.

His boys arrived, greeting us politely. I made small talk to avert attention from the unease of the pastor's presence.

"You're a good batsman," I said to the young Timothy. "Perhaps you'll play for Australia one day."

"I want to play for India, like Sashin," he countered, pulling his Indian cricket cap around for me to see. Sashin Tendulkar is one of the greatest cricketers ever and he was on the top of his game in 1999. Any kid would want to bat like he did. Still, the boy's identification as Indian came as yet another surprise.

"But you are from Australia," I said.

The boy seemed confused.

"I am from dust."

Staines laughed.

"Yes, you are. Now go wash the dust off your hands and grab some lunch. We have to go."

As the boys ran off, Staines explained that Timothy was referring to the Bible's teaching that God made us from the dust of the earth.

"Dust to dust. See you later."

Of course, I didn't think anything of his last words at the time.

Staines went off happily, still laughing at his son. The pastor did not. He continued to stare at me accusingly, no doubt waiting for me to go. Eventually, my discomfort grew sufficiently to warrant some action, some comment.

"Maybe I'm just interested in his work."

Only then did the pastor leave me, but not before a final withering judgement.

"And maybe you'll start hugging lepers."

I had one more encounter worth mentioning before I left the Compound that day. Actually two.

The first occurred as I made some reconnaissance of the house. The building was modest; large by village standards, but not extravagant. Practical is a word that comes to mind. A flat-roofed construction with a pleasant aspect adorned with a metal cross in the bars above the front alcove. Behind the house was a courtyard with a low verandahed building on two sides consisting of accommodation for workers and visitors, as well as store rooms. Further on from the house, open to the main area of the compound, was a shelter for the vehicles and a workshop space.

Anyway, Mrs Staines and her children, including the older daughter, Esther, were eating their lunch on the steps at the front of the house, watching the packing of the vehicles. Apparently Philip and Timothy were to travel with Staines to the event in Monoharpur.

As I was off to one side behind some plants I was able to observe Mrs Staines for the first time a little more closely. Of course, there was nothing unusual in the normal motherly affection that a woman has for her children. There was some banter about going on the camp - in fact, Timothy asked her to go with them.

As the children left, taking their plates with them to the kitchen - I noted their willing obedience - I came into view and cheerfully greeted her. And this was what I felt worth narrating.

Her countenance changed. She took her time. She looked directly at me.

"You're a journalist."

I started to reply, hoping to strike up a conversation. She stopped me.

"Leave my children out of it."

It was blunt, it was direct and it left me in no doubt that there were deeper feelings of fear and distrust towards me than Staines had let on. The expectation that I was there to expose their activities was made clear in her reference to 'it', and that my reporting could be harmful to her children, or that I would be so crass as to use the children to harm Staines. Unfortunately, she was right. That is who I was.

The second encounter is noteworthy because it led to the next stage of my investigation and to an incident that torments me still, an incident that creeps up on me and confronts me at unexpected moments, an incident that harangues me, hankering for, even demanding a justification, hoping for a rationalisation, but at least a judgement, even if that be a condemnation.

It was the departure of Champa, the woman rejected by Staines, sent on her way into the wilderness.

In her rejection surely she would be a worthwhile source of information now. I made to follow.

I was interrupted by the two Staines boys, Philip and Timothy, who arrived with chai and biscuits. For me.

I could not, would not, reject their hospitality and kindness, so at odds with the former encounter with the mother. As my quarry slipped away I sipped chai and ate biscuits.

"Please thank your mother for me. It is most kind."

And strange.

"It was Tim's idea," said the older.

"I saw you didn't have any lunch," said the younger.

The kindness of children. And the mother had allowed it, in spite of what she had said to me.

These people kept surprising me.

But it was time to pursue my next lead. Champa had disappeared, of course, but I knew where to find her.

Or so I thought.

EVIDENCE AND ANGER

I retrieved my scooter, Mishra's scooter to be more correct, and made my way out to the village where Champa lived, or had lived to be more correct again.

I fully expected to see her on the way, knowing that she could not have travelled too far, but of her there was no sign. I didn't know that I would never see her again. I know nothing of her and I know not her fate. But I didn't know any of that as I made my way out on the dusty road.

I soon accepted that she had taken a different route and I had missed her, but I continued on to the village to speak to her husband and wait for her there.

As I drew closer it was smoke rising from the village that next attracted my attention.

Champa's husband, Bhartu, was ripping the last of his sheaves of rice away from his burning crop. I leapt to assist him, but there was not much left to do. Most of his crop, his food for the year, painstakingly teased from the soil, was now smoke and ash.

We hauled the little that had been saved into his small house to prevent further retaliation. As it was, he would need to leave the village to seek work to avoid starvation later in the year.

I discovered then that his wife had left him without saying where she was going. The night before some men had entered their house and beaten them as they lay on their cot, leaving them bruised and afraid. Champa had bound his arm where he had received what was possibly a bone-breaking blow when trying to defend himself. She made a poultice for his bruises, gently easing his pain.

She was gone in the morning.

And today almost his entire crop had been burnt.

Leprosy was still a terrifying curse in rural India. But I was a journalist. I asked questions.

Although he could not be sure, Bhartu, the husband, suspected that one of the men who had beaten them was his own brother.

Why?

Leprosy? Yes, people were afraid of it. So was I. Irrationally. But these reactions were extreme.

Of course, there was a time, long ago, when extreme reactions were necessary. Contracting leprosy meant no cure and no hope; leprosy was a curse and a danger to the entire community.

One belief was that the more extreme the suffering in this life for the sinner, the greater the chance of a better reincarnation. The practice was to bury the leper - alive - to increase the suffering and ensure a better future life.

It buried the infection also.

But in 1999 this was no longer the practice, neither was beating a man and his wife, even if she was a leper.

Interestingly, the brother stood to acquire the land that Bhartu farmed should Bhartu no longer be able to do so. But even that motivation seemed insufficient to me and I wondered if there was more to it.

As I sympathised with Bhartu over his misfortunes, I confess I was not all 'love and charity'. I still had a job to do. I still felt fear and aversion at the thought of leprosy. I still desperately wanted evidence on Staines.

I suggested that he convert to Christianity.

He seemed alarmed.

"Staines can help you; protect you," I said.

"Not out here."

Surely, I argued, there were Christians around, if not in his village, then surrounding villages. A conversion in exchange for protection would have been useful - for both of us.

He was adamant.

"The village elders will decide."

Decide what?

His fate, his life, his ownership, his wife? Community brings many benefits, but it can be an immovable overlord.

A village meeting had been called that evening. I intended to be present. There had to be more to this story.

Back at the hospital, Shanti seemed to be doing well. Her blood type had been rare - B negative - difficult to find, but the bleeding had slowed and she was feeling better. Of course, her focus was our baby. I tried to keep my distractions at bay when I was with her.

She had previously asked me about a name for our baby. I had not, and could not now give it serious thought.

"I like *Vardanuja*," she said.

And so it was, and is. 'Gift of life' is a good name, a reminder that life is indeed a gift, and as I was too well aware with Shanti's condition, it was a fragile gift, for a time only.

The doctor was also cautiously pleased with Shanti's progress, although he warned that surgery may be necessary and the city hospital was the much preferred option should that be the case. Of course, he also warned that moving her could be dangerous. And there was a cost.

I was grateful for his help, but he insisted that the body healed itself. All he could do was assist.

I took the opportunity to ask about his work with the patients at the Leprosy Home, and asked if he had treated Champa.

"Yes, probably. If she's there, I treat her."

But he didn't remember the many names.

I mentioned that she had been sent back to her village. Did he know why?

I wondered silently whether Staines had told me all there was to know.

"You'd have to ask Graham," he said, not being drawn in.

"You know Staines?"

"Of course."

I moved in - too quickly.

"Is he into conversion?"

"He's a missionary."

The doctor seemed to think it was obvious Staines would be 'into' conversion. But was he 'forcing' conversion? I wasn't quite ready to ask that. After all, the doctor was treating patients at the Leprosy Home, and no doubt doing good business.

"So, effectively, he hates other religions?" I asked.

"Hate? No, I don't think so... he doesn't take *prasad*, but 'hate'?"

"Has he tried to convert you?"

"Always," he laughed.

The realisation hit me. Staines' friends, not his enemies, could be the answer: they were the people with whom Staines let down his guard, they were the people he most wanted to convert, but they were also the people most loyal to him.

"That's against the law," I said, my mind processing this new idea and my mouth revealing that process without prejudice.

"The law?"

His tone had changed, and so had his body language, but I was at least one step behind. Oh, I still had much to learn.

"Yes, he tries to convert you and gives you work at the Leprosy Home - that's inducement."

Too late I detected my mistake.

"I can make my own decision about conversion. I do not need inducement. No inducement brings real conversion anyway."

"But the missionaries..."

"He tries to persuade me. And I try to persuade him. Debate. No inducement."

The conversation was over.

I mumbled an apology and the doctor made it clear where his allegiance lay.

"Graham Staines is my friend."

That evening I was back among his enemies; safer ground I thought. And so began the incident, that incident, the incident that one moment condemns me and mocks me the next, the incident that won't leave me alone, perhaps the single strongest influence in me writing all this, right now.

I was back in that village - Bhartu and Champa's village.

A large fire had been built in the centre of the communal area. The elders passed a pot of rice beer from one to the other. All the men of the village had gathered and more besides. Not only did they have a personal interest in the proceedings, but it was a spectacle that did not often occur.

And like them, I was there.

I watched unnoticed from the shadows as Bhartu shuffled forward into the dancing firelight to face the judgement.

His arm was in a rough sling and he walked carefully with the aid of a stick - he was no fool to the ways of men, I thought. He wanted to give the impression that he had been punished enough for the misdemeanour of having a wife who had contracted leprosy.

The elders were not unreasonable, given their context. Bhartu's defence was that Champa had been cured, but he could not prove this and he had to admit that he was only going on the words of the missionary.

They were afraid. In their understanding she was not cured, but cursed, and now she may have visited that curse upon them. Again. What was more, she had drawn water from the village well and they now had to have that cleansed, at great cost, before anyone could draw water from it again - a process for which Bhartu certainly could not afford to pay.

The accusations were clear and convincing. Bhartu had been irresponsible in the extreme. He should have consulted the village elders before taking her back. He should not have taken her back. He should not have believed the missionary.

All that was reasonable, I thought. But the crowd was vocal and hostile and unreasonable. The process was constantly interrupted by shouts and jeers. Like a jealous volcano spouting odd plumes of gas, impatiently wanting to erupt, the crowd, or at least certain anonymous members of the crowd, was angry and calling for consequences.

Finally, one of the elders asked if anyone would speak for Bhartu.

He turned to the gathered village expectantly.

Nobody came forward.

Some were looking down, unable to look up and meet Bhartu's shocked gaze.

It was confirmed.

The fear of leprosy was real, but there was more going on. Political agendas no doubt.

The next question asked clearly shocked Bhartu.

"Does anyone want him to stay in the village."

The same voices immediately took up the cry of condemnation. I could see others who did not concur, but clearly could not risk the confrontation. They had to continue living here, in the community. I did not.

I stepped through the crowd and into the light.

"I will speak for him."

Everyone stared at me. Of course, many had seen me earlier and would no doubt have heard of my visits.

A man in the crowd stood - I had seen him before. I couldn't place him immediately, but later the face emerged from my memory - he was in the group who had been taunting the pastor on my first visit to the marketplace, the day I first saw Staines when he picked up the leper boy.

His name was Mahendra.

"He's not from the village."

Ironically, neither was he.

I greeted them politely, gave my name and told them I was a journalist.

Again Mahendra protested, but I spoke over him, making an enemy of my own.

"The government clinics and hospitals provide medicines that heal other diseases. You accept those treatments. Why not this one?"

Mahendra attacked, verbally, "This one is working for the missionary," drawing a rumble of animosity from his supporters.

But this time, an Elder intervened, "Mahendra. Let him speak."

I continued quickly.

"The government medicines have cured Bhartu's wife. They say he should take her back."

Mahendra was not so easily silenced, "It was the missionary who said she is cured."

"The government will agree with the missionary," I countered.

"Ha!" Mahendra gloated. "The government does what the missionaries want."

He had a point and normally I would have agreed with him, but my high school debating training was asserting itself and I was not so easily beaten.

"Then why do you blame Bhartu?"

The argument was simple but effective. Why indeed?

But Mahendra was not seeking truth or a fair outcome. He had an agenda, a political one. So he went on the attack again.

"You are a Christian."

"I am speaking for this man."

"You argue like the missionaries, you talk like the missionaries...

"No..."

He turned to the crowd.

"This one will write in his newspaper that you are all fools, ignorant farmers."

I tried to interrupt, sensing the influence he already had with this crowd. Mahendra rolled on, incensing them with the supposed insults I would level at them in print, and convincing them that I would use their apparent 'stupidity' to take their autonomy.

"Then he will have the government forcing you to take the cursed woman back."

In that moment I felt their frustration. These people lived a simple existence. Their community was their life, for the most part. The antics and actions of the modern world, of governments, of politicians, perhaps of missionaries, often left them stranded, confused, helpless and afraid. By 1999, many millions of farmers had already left the villages and drifted to the cities, families and lives destroyed.

But I did not have time to ponder this social conundrum.

Most of the crowd were on their feet. The mood had changed rapidly and radically.

"Unless we stop him," Mahendra cried, "Stop him from writing these lies!"

I had my back to the fire and members of the crowd were already moving towards me, shouting sentiments about me such as 'beating' and 'cleansing'.

It was an ugly situation that was getting uglier. I don't mind admitting that I was afraid.

I ripped my notepad from my shoulder bag, yelling for them to listen.

"Listen to what I have written."

I lifted my notepad, reading quickly before Mahendra had a chance to press his advantage.

"The traditional lifestyle in the villages is disintegrating. Farmers are leaving their land and families. Why?"

Mahendra gave me the answer, unwittingly I am sure.

"The missionaries!"

"Yes!" I responded with equal vigour, and continued reading.

"Missionaries have been operating across India for hundreds of years now, and they have undermined thousands of years of tradition. Converts to Christianity no longer respect feast days, make sacrifices to the village gods or submit to the village elders."

They were listening.

"No wonder there is social failure. But do the missionaries get the blame?"

The crowd were responding now - no, the missionaries did not get the blame.

"Exactly. Nobody blames them. Missionaries divide and conquer, causing the people of India to fight each other. But that is like attacking the chickens when they do not lay eggs. It is the snake who is disturbing the chickens that must be destroyed. When a snake is taking the eggs or the chicks you do not attack the chickens; you lay in wait for the snake and you cut off its head."

Well, some beliefs would not agree with this, but these farmers identified with the idea at least. I had won them over.

An insignificant incident? Were you expecting more?

Ah, but ideas and words can be dangerous.

These may not have been my exact words, but near enough. I had nothing written on the page, of course. I was making it up to save myself, and it worked. I think I finished with something like, "The people of India need to protect their traditions by destroying these snakes, the true enemies of a successful India."

As I made my way out of there, back to the hospital where I could hold my baby and see my wife, where I could feel relief flood my body and shake in safety as the adrenalin wore off, as I disappeared into the dark to find my scooter, I heard Mahendra's voice above the rest, intense, tenacious...

"We must cut the head off the snake!"

I can still hear it.

MONOHARPUR

At the time, of course, it meant nothing. Words. Just words. It was Staines who disagreed with me on that, but I'll get to that.

Shanti was stable, but the doctor was still concerned. He wanted to move her to a bigger hospital. He feared a need for surgery - a hysterectomy, I suppose. I had no idea and didn't ask. The doctor wasn't well equipped to perform the surgery should it be needed.

For me, only me, to decide: embrace the risk of moving her - bleeding en route could be fatal - or to linger in uncertainty?

And the cost. Always the cost.

Staines was out of town, my leads had dried up, and I needed something to keep me occupied. I was an impatient young man, sailing around in circles, waiting for something to happen.

I spoke to Mishra, offering to write about the woman, Champa, and the methods I suspected Staines of using.

He was disdainful.

"How is that going to help your conversion?"

It wasn't.

I tried another tack.

"What about the angry villagers? Perhaps I could make them seem unreasonable. That would please the Christians."

"Banerjee," he said, "I'm paying you to convert. That's it."

"But Sir, I still need to act like a journalist."

"Then write about something else!"

I was angry. I was tired. I was helpless.

Of course Mishra knew more than he was letting on. I can't prove all of it, of course, but his was more than an editor's interest in finding evidence. Yes, his argument made enough sense, but even now I suspect there was even more motivating him than I later discovered.

These meanderings of thought are irrelevant to the situation back then. I needed to do something, and my options were to convert, or to convert. No option.

I went to find Staines.

And as he, Staines, had said - Monoharpur was on the other side of the mountain, and way off in the foothills. There was hardly a road to the place. The mountains referred to are the Eastern Ghats - at this point high enough and difficult enough to have avoided human habitation. This section of the Ghats hosts one of the few remaining tiger reserves - Similipal. Monoharpur was off to the south of this largely inaccessible and imposing monument to a very old India.

It was about as remote as it gets in India: no facilities, no electricity, no police, no modern influences... just a few people eking a living out of the land. This was the lifestyle that I so romantically thought I should be defending. While not denying some of its charm, it is, in truth, a tough existence.

Religion is the only way of life in such places. There were signs of it everywhere - shrines, symbols, offerings to the gods. And so it was in Monoharpur, when I eventually found the place - a scattering of houses, packed close, a few paddies undulating outwards, then forest.

The few 'faithful' had gathered for the jungle camp from the surrounding area. I say 'few' because there are comparatively few Christians in India, around two percent of the population. Although some states have a significantly higher percentage, Orissa is not one of them.

Monoharpur boasted a church building, indicating a livelier Christian presence in this village. Not that it looked any different from the other small houses lining the red kuccha track, but a dedicated building nonetheless, distinguished by the small cross above the door outside.

The mission vehicles were parked alongside, one acting as a mobile clinic from which Staines tended to the sick. Philip and Timothy were playing cricket again with the local children - a perennial pastime.

"I didn't expect to see you out here," was his opening line.

What was I to say to that? I mumbled something about research.

I don't remember all we said and spoke of - the conversation came and went - but I developed a respect for the man in that short time that coloured my perception significantly. I still thought of him as a fanatic - I still do - but it's a different kind of fanatic to what I had imagined; not all bad.

I remember, for example, that I asked him *why* he did this, why he was a missionary.

"It's my calling," he said.

Whatever that means.

But he also showed me an old photo - black and white originally, but now faded to sepia, frayed and bent. He pulled it out of his wallet. The photo was of a boy, perhaps 16 years of age, the terrible testimony to his leprosy protruding from his neck and lower jaw.

"When I was 16, the lady who ran the mission back then visited our church in Australia. She showed us this photo. I couldn't get it out of my mind: a boy, my age, with no hope."

Staines was definitely a missionary of the hazardous variety. There was no money piling up back in Australia for each convert he made. There was no god-like worship of him such as an ego-maniac might thrive on. There was no political gain for him personally. He would not have stayed so long - 35 years in that place - if he didn't really believe in what he was doing.

And I couldn't help liking him.

One moment smiling, the next deeply, genuinely, concerned about the suffering of others. He even started teasing me about helping him - an opportunity for me to get closer to 'converting' you may think - but he was squeezing puss from an infected wound on some unfortunate boy at the time. I couldn't even look!

I'd moved on to asking why he needed to stay on in India, since the government now provided the medicines for leprosy that were previously unavailable. Of course, the answer was right in front of my eyes, and he enjoyed making me watch him do something I was not prepared nor able to do myself.

But he was self-deprecating - at the time I was still distrusting; now I believe it was his genuine humility. I mentioned the boy I'd seen him pick up in the market place, citing his lack of fear.

He laughed, and told me of the first time he'd picked up a suffering leper...

"I nearly threw up I was so scared. Or maybe it was just the curry."

He laughed. He looked out into the distance - brilliant acting, or genuine recall?

"I was riding my bike when I passed this man - or what was left of him - lying on the side of the road waiting for death. I tried to ride on, but God wouldn't let me."

He looked directly at me.

"Now we have a medical cure. You could do it."

No, I couldn't. He was definitely having fun with me.

It struck me later that the first time he picked up a leper, there was no cure!

Staines was also no fool - in time he manoeuvred me onto the topic of the pastor, David, and what I had written about the conversion of the tribal girl.

I dismissed my writing as 'words, just words.' And this was where he disagreed with me. Suddenly serious, he argued quite strongly that words mattered greatly, perhaps more than anything.

"Words are power," he said, "they contain ideas, truth…"

I did not remember then, but I remember now, other words. Words I spoke. Words I uttered without thought or knowledge. Words that visit me still, unbidden in unexpected moments.

But I digress again.

I remembered that he was a missionary.

"So you help people, so that they will convert," I said.

"People choose," he said.

"But your purpose is not to help them; it is to convert them."

"I help people because God loves them."

"But they will naturally feel grateful, so they will listen, and you can persuade them - especially uneducated people."

I remember he smiled.

"If only. Jesus healed ten lepers once. How many do you think came back to thank him?"

I sensed he was about to demolish my argument.

"Not all, I suppose."

"One. One out of ten. But he still healed all of them."

I watched the children playing cricket for a while after that. At the time it was a distraction; now it is one of my most painful memories. Because those boys were good.

I'm not talking about cricket. I'm talking about them as people. I'm no expert on children, but I have some experience now and one sees, at times, beautiful compassion; at times, indifferent cruelty. No doubt they were the same. No doubt they had their moments of struggle with selfishness. No doubt my view is skewed. But the few snapshots I had of Philip and Timothy were all of compassion.

Particularly on this occasion. Exceptional, unprovoked compassion. Although I thought very differently at first.

The children had divided themselves into teams. I watched Timothy clean bowl the last batsman of the opposing team. Apparently. Celebrations and commiserations were in play, but Timothy would have none of it.

"What about Lahki? He hasn't batted," I heard him say.

"He can't bat," was the retort.

"You only need two runs to win."

A huddled discussion ensued, and Lahki was brought out to bat. An ironic name when you consider the English pronunciation: 'lucky'. The boy had unfortunate karma - cerebral palsy of some sort, I suppose. He walked with a bobbing wobble, knees clashing, one arm permanently jutting out from the body. He could hardly hold a bat, let alone run. He looked terrified.

Philip moved in close to the batsman, ready to swoop on an easy catch. Timothy moved back to his bowling start.

I was appalled. I thought about how cruel children can be in that moment. And the British and their callous rules of fairness. The game wasn't over until everybody had batted. Those were the rules. And here they were closing in on this poor unfortunate for an easy dismissal to the shame of this terrified villager.

I was filling with self-righteous anger and reminded of my cause.

Then Timothy was running in to bowl. But at the last moment he slowed and sent a placid looping ball down the pitch. Lahki didn't have to bat - the ball hit the bat, dribbling off to one side.

Philip yelled, "Run Lahki, run!"

How can they be so mean, I thought.

Lahki toddled off down the pitch as Philip easily picked up the ball and swivelling grandly he whipped the ball back to Timothy at the wicket. But the throw was wide.

By the time another fielder had retrieved the ball, Lahki had completed one 'run'. He was toddling back for another - the winning run!

By now, Philip was running alongside him, urging him on.

I was confused.

But there was plenty of time to still get him out - it was like prolonging the torture.

Somehow Timothy fumbled the catch from the fielder, scrambling around ridiculously as if he couldn't even see it. Finally he had it in hand and hurled it as hard as he could to the other end - way too hard. And wide! Again!

His hands went to his head in horror. The wicket keeper was in shock - he couldn't have got near it.

And then Lahki was home. He had won the game for his team. They were all cheering. Lakhi was the hero, the boy who hit the winning runs against the odds.

I cannot describe the look on that boy's face. I am not even going to try. It moves me every time I think of it.

Of course, those boys, Philip and Timothy, had intended this to happen - what a gift to a crippled boy.

I felt shame. Shame at what I had assumed, imagined, believed. Perhaps this event, more than any other, turned my beliefs about Staines. A man who teaches his children to be like that... I only hope I can do half as well.

Staines joined me. I made a feeble joke about his children doing 'good'. "Could be seen as inducement," I said. Of course it is an absurd suggestion, but I was in fact, close to reality. Any kindness can be inducement. Indeed, had not I used something similar? That girl who was baptised - I tried to claim that her signature in her Bible was evidence of coercion, of being 'forced'.

I moved onto the subject of karma. I was no sage, no expert on religious beliefs, but the concept of karma runs deep in the psyche. It makes sense. So it was all fine and good that Staines helped people whose karma had visited trouble upon them, but he went way beyond that: Staines was trying to reverse the effect of the karma and surely that would only prolong the suffering. The karma was still there, waiting, deserved, and ready to be inflicted, whether in this life or the next.

Staines was confident.

"You can call leprosy 'karma' if you like, but what we do in response - that is not karma. Take Sundar, for example. Refusing to accept that he's still alive is not his karma - what *we do* in response to suffering is not *his* karma."

"But people are afraid of the curse, afraid that they may be inflicted with his karma," I responded, no doubt inadequately.

"So fear, unfounded fear, drives them to do evil instead of good?"

I really didn't know enough to have a powerful religious argument, but the conversation was congenial. I was relaxed: 'cool, calm and collected' as they say. And my journalism had taught me a little about asking questions and turning an argument.

"But what you do is 'good'?" I asked.

"Yeah, I hope so."

"And your 'good' converts people."

"Sometimes."

"And then you are free to do more so-called 'good' for those people because they have converted."

At this point I switched subjects, and this I remember well, for it was the first time I saw a crack in him.

I told him about my wife, in hospital.

"The doctor advised a transfer to the city for surgery. I can't afford to pay for it."

Staines was silent. He knew that I was asking for help.

I waited.

Eventually he said the obvious, the standard response.

"There are so many needs, so many people who need something. Our policy is not to give money, but to do what we can instead."

"What if I convert to Christianity?"

He looked at me then, unsure of my sincerity.

"That could be considered a 'forced' conversion," he said.

"So fear, unfounded fear, prevents you from doing good."

And there was the crack.

His own words used against him. For the first time I felt I was winning, whichever way it went.

"I'll pray about it," he said, and made to return to his makeshift clinic.

I was smiling inside.

"Why don't you check out the preaching. There's a good crowd today," he said as he walked away.

I did.

And what I saw chilled me, stunted my smile, unsettled me deeply. If only I had understood.

I saw... Mahendra.

There was no avoiding him. He, along with two others, were leaving the gathering when I approached.

"Ah, it's the lawyer," he said.

Sarcasm. It didn't ease my feelings of unease.

"What are you doing here?" I asked.

"Don't be nervous."

"I'm not. Just surprised to see you here, that's all."

"Are you sure you not Christian?" he asked.

I was getting over my shock at seeing him; I think I was quickly getting annoyed at his... I think 'cockiness' is the right word.

"What if I was?"

He was very good at controlling a situation. He smiled impassively back at me for a while. Long enough to cause me to speak again.

"Nothing?" I asked.

"It was you who said we shouldn't blame the chickens. Just cut the head off the snake."

I felt chilled again. It was not the words so much. They were still just words to me. It was the way he said it.

"What are you doing?" I asked again.

"Performing a drama. Want to come?"

He didn't wait for a reply. He and his cronies moved off without a backward glance and I drifted toward the gathering.

I remember vaguely hearing the preacher's words, echoed by an interpreter:

"Blessed are those who are persecuted because of righteousness, for theirs is the kingdom of God."

Even then I recognised the words - part of something Jesus said known as the sermon on the mount. But they meant nothing to me at the time - my mind was on Mahendra.

Nothing at the time. But now. Now I find it uncanny, a coincidence that only adds to my frustration and guilt and confusion. What curious meaning those words hold. What strange reality they portended.

But as I said, at the time, I was not thinking about words. I was watching Mahendra disappear into the surrounding forest. I decided to follow him.

The path they chose led through deep forest and over some steep ridges. I was careful to keep my distance and remained out of sight. I knew I was potentially stepping into danger and certainly questioned the wisdom of the action I was taking. The imagination does unusual things when one's sense of danger is heightened, but I consoled myself that no tigers would be found this far south of Similipal. Snakes were another matter.

Tracking the men was easy, even for a city boy like me. They made no effort to hide their progress. Eventually I heard other voices - they had reached their destination.

I crept forward very carefully, keeping low, constantly checking for snakes as I did so. We had reached a point close to the 'road' again, which meandered around the ridges as it coiled between villages.

I considered walking up to the group. What was there to be afraid of? I was not close enough to hear what they were saying, but close enough to notice that Mahendra was distributing alcohol. Something made me cautious. In truth, I was fearful. After all, Mahendra had recently threatened me at the village when I stood up for Bhartu. It was still fresh in my memory.

And now? How do I feel now? Should I have done something? Was that my opportunity? Oh, I had Shanti and Vardanuja to think of, yes. But that does nothing to stop the questions and accusations in my mind. I didn't know. I keep telling myself I didn't know. But it's not enough.

I crept away and made my way back to Monoharpur. I found myself shaking gently. I had been in a state of high alert the entire time. I rested on a ridge which gave a view in both directions, as if I had been stalked by a silent storm and had now been whipped up on a high wave, waiting, helpless, to be sent sailing down one side or the other, into the deep below, not knowing which side would drive me to greater depth, which side would blow me into the brunt of the blast, which side would have the waves washing over me.

Of course, I really didn't know anything back then. I just had this terrible feeling of unease. Something was not right, but perhaps that was to be expected. Staines was creating disruption. Conversions cause concern and confusion, upset and alarm.

My own experience with Mahendra was no doubt colouring my judgement and causing me to feel more tension than was warranted.

I surveyed the landscape from my wavetop, but I could not see beneath the undulating tree tops, or on the far rice paddies, or in the far shacks and houses. All was at peace at that distance. Like looking at a human being - who can see into the heart?

Evil intentions were hidden beneath the facade.

I returned to Monoharpur where Staines was entertaining Philip and Timothy on his bicycle, pushing them around on it. He was in a jovial mood.

When he saw me he laughed and offered me water.

"You like going for long walks," he said. It hadn't escaped his attention that I had been missing for a while. But his natural and serious, yet also relaxed, interest in others was attractive. It pacified resistance.

Somehow, seeing him caused me concern again. I suppose I knew something was about to happen, but I had not yet worked out what that was. Why did I not see it? What more should or could I have done?

"Do you ever worry that you might be in danger out here?" I asked.

"Yeah, from diarrhoea," he laughed. "Out here we don't get Delhi belly. It's much worse; we get Orissa orifice."

I smiled along with him. Philip made a small noise, like passing wind, causing Timothy to giggle. I'm told boys that age enjoy jokes about bodily functions.

"Have you heard of a man called Mahendra?"

It was a question that potentially exposed me, a question that shifted me from anti-missionary to pro Mr Staines, if not pro-missionary. It was not calculated as a step toward my 'conversion', although I would have argued that line if Mishra had questioned me.

No, it was that Mahendra had scared me, and still did.

But my fear had no evidential basis. Staines was apparently not reading my concern, or perhaps he was still suspicious of my real intentions. Rightly so.

"Which one?" he asked.

Of course it was a fairly common name in the region. It was a foolish question.

"He doesn't like missionaries," I said.

He looked at me - I thought for a moment he was going to say "like you?" but he didn't. He was still smiling.

"Well, being a missionary's not a popularity contest."

Then for a moment he was serious: "Have you heard something?"

"I'm not certain."

"Mr Banerjee, only two things in life are certain. Death and taxes." He laughed. I think he often laughed at his own jokes.

And then, his serious side slipped in as he added: "It's worth being ready for both."

And the thing is, I think he was - ready, that is. It's one of the things that alleviates my guilt when the accusations come. Not that he was aware of anything specific - he would never have kept his boys with him if he had known of any danger. Only the year before he had ended a jungle camp early when the police had warned of potential trouble. His faith was apparently practical. But from the little I saw, his faith also freed him to be relaxed and at ease with the world around him. Perhaps I'm overstating... I know memory plays tricks on one and I had so little to go on. This is merely my impression, some years since.

I could end my recollection there - it would be a powerful final moment with the man, but these were not his last words to me.

He had some advice for me.

By this time he had loaded the bicycle on the back of his vehicle and he was about to drive away, Timothy on his lap, excited at being allowed to steer.

"Your wife just had a baby."

He paused as he looked at me.

"Don't work so hard; get back to your family."

I said I would.

"See you later," he said.

FIRE AND FORGIVENESS

By the time I had made my way along the 20 kilometres of dirt track back to Thakarmunda and the main road to Baripada, the sun was setting on the world and mist was descending from the surrounding hills.

I was hungry and tired. I was thinking about Staines. Yes, I was less suspicious of him now, but I had to remember that he was still a missionary. I had to align my thinking, gain perspective...

I found a meal and ruminated on the experiences of the day. 'Conversion' for me was looking increasingly possible. It was the missionaries blind spot, I realised. They would almost always take a risk on a conversion. Infiltrating the Christian group was not going to be a problem.

But it required a strong will and pure commitment to the cause. I would eventually betray people with whom I was engaging in relationship. This did not appeal to me. I really was starting to like the man, and his children.

And who was to say I would not eventually be swayed by their beliefs myself. What if I started doubting my convictions? What then? No, I needed to be so convinced of my cause, so convinced that Christianity was bringing destruction, so convinced that the Christians were deceived or intentionally malicious, that I would be prepared to deceive, betray, dismiss and destroy them.

Was I ready to do that? Determined enough to do that? Convinced enough to do that?

By the time I had ruminated sufficiently both on my meal and the thoughts circling in my mind, but never settling, the ride back to Baripada in the cold did not appeal. Shanti was in the hospital - I could not give her better care. I may have mentioned before that I was young and foolish. Of course, I didn't know the future. Would I have decided differently had I known? Of course. A thousand times differently. But I didn't know. I wish I had taken Staines' advice.

But I didn't. I wasn't ready to leave the scene at Monoharpur and felt it best to go back the following day. It made no sense to ride all the way back to Baripada, then back again the next morning. So it was that I borrowed a blanket at the police station and lay down on a bench to see the night out in Thakarmunda.

Dawn.

A new day. So often we see the dawning of a new day in positive terms - hope, opportunity, ...

But sometimes...

Have you ever felt it would be better if the sun didn't rise? Better if the world just stopped turning for a moment so we could repair something; stop the world and sort it out; make right that which has gone wrong?

The cyclists arrived at the police station at dawn. I woke to the sound of a bicycle clattering to the ground, then anxious voices, then a man choking on his words, then raw emotion emerging, obstructing the utterance, rousing me rapidly from my drowsiness. I stumbled into the room to hear... to hear... but not to believe. At first.

I could not keep pace with the police van on the track to Monoharpur. And all the while the sun kept on climbing the sky on my left.

What to tell you? I'm sure you read about it or heard the story somewhere. At the time, all we had was a man and his two sons who had gone to sleep in one of the two vehicles, parked near the church at Monoharpur. Youths from surrounding villages were celebrating a traditional *Danghri* dance some 100 metres away, giving themselves to the rhythm of the leather drums, the chant, the stamp and sway around the large fire. A group of men entered the village, carrying lit torches and apparently fuel. They silently locked or barricaded some doors of houses where they apparently knew friends of Staines were sleeping. They surrounded the vehicles, adding straw, fuel, and finally attacked, smashing, lighting... preventing the occupants from escaping the flames.

Nobody from the village came to their aid. Although arguably, few knew what was happening.

One man, a mission worker, on finding his door locked, knocked a hole in the roof of the house and came running with a bucket of water. He was severly beaten for his efforts, whereupon he ran to get help from other villagers. All too late.

This man was still weeping when I arrived. He sat on the ground, bruised and dirty, staring at the burnt out frames of the vehicles. I wonder if he still feels the guilt and torment I feel? But what more could he have done? He was one man against at least forty.

Staines was heard yelling at one point, "Let the children go."

They didn't.

Instead they shouted "*maro, maro...*" - "beat them, beat them..." and "*zindabad, zindabad...*" - "victory, victory..."

When they were satisfied that the vehicles and their occupants were truly 'beaten', the group departed, undeterred, back into the forest, dispersing to their various homes and villages, leaving the burnt out vehicles and the bodies, charred beyond recognition, huddled together in death.

There is an English saying: 'the elephant in the room'. We can talk about what happened, but there is an elephant in the room which I cannot avoid. Where is god when such things happen? More precisely, where was Staines' god when this happened?

All of it - the scene, the car, the remains - was chilling: blackened, burned, charred. Even so, there was one thing that truly gripped me by the throat. As I circled what was now a crime scene, I saw something near the vehicle, a small mound, soot-coloured. As I moved around, part of it seared and burned, but some of it intact, I recognised it. An Indian cricket team cap. Timothy's cap. Somehow, it must have fallen out of the vehicle. Perhaps he was wearing it and it was knocked from his head in an attempt to escape. I don't want to think about it. But there it is. It still looks me in the eye, challenging me to accept what was before me, staring me down, down, down...

I remembered my own words, the words Mahendra had taken up: "We must cut the head off the snake!" Actually, he shouted the words, venomously: "WE MUST CUT THE HEAD OFF THE SNAKE!"

Was this the drama he meant? Yes, today we know it was exactly what he meant, and the authorities have done their work - he is now incarcerated for his crimes. But at the time I had nothing concrete to go on. In the midst of my confusion I remembered that I was a journalist and that I had a job to do. At least that gave me focus as I tried to take in what had happened.

Yes, Staines was involved in the conversion of tribals, the unscheduled people groups of that rural area. He was a missionary. The tribals were frustrated. Converts were not respecting village elders. But was Staines converting illegally? I still had no evidence of that.

And the kids? Blaming the children for the sins of the father. Why!? Let them go! What harm can they do? What harm have they done? They played cricket.

Karma?

No. What we do to people is not their karma. How can it be? It can only contribute to our karma, if there is such a thing.

And god? Surely any god, by definition, is able to prevent such a thing? But god didn't. Therefore god chose to let it happen.

Of course, such speculation happens over time. Even now, years later, I ask the questions. At the time, I raced back to Baripada.

I went first to the hospital. I needed to talk to Shanti, my wife. Young as she was, she always calmed me. Her unwavering faith in me stabilised and sustained me. I needed her now. I needed to take some of the shock and emotion out of my reporting. I needed perspective.

Shanti was not in her bed.

Someone else was.

I panicked.

Eventually I found her. I found her lying on a blanket on the floor, curled around Vardanuja.

I held back my tears of relief. Even my tears of anger.

I paid for a bed.

I could tell she had been hurt by moving around. She didn't say anything, but I could tell.

I called Mishra, but his office told me he was already on his way to Baripada. The news had broken of the attack. At the time, all that had been reported was that vehicles had been burnt. With Mishra on his way I needed to get to work or I had no chance of him paying for Shanti's hospital needs.

I wanted to stay by her bedside. I wanted to care for her. I wanted to hold my baby. But…

I was on my way to the Mission Compound when a vehicle forced me from the road with much pressing of the horn. Mishra.

"Where have you been, Banerjee? Do you have an article written?"

My first impulse was to ask why he hadn't paid for Shanti's bed. I said nothing.

"Get in," he ordered.

I did as I was told, climbing into the passenger seat next to him. He waited for me to speak first.

"He's been murdered," I said.

"Staines?"

I nodded.

"Then not 'murdered'. He was killed for converting tribals."

"But Sir, the man…"

"He must have done something. Provoked it somehow."

"There's no evidence."

"Find some. Conversions. Inducements. People will talk now. We need an article by deadline today. This is front page news - your opportunity."

I could stand it no longer. A man and his two sons had just been burnt to death and it was viewed as an 'opportunity'. I was not yet so hardened. I removed myself from the vehicle.

Mishra leaned out of the window.

"Have you been converted so easily, Banerjee?"

"Sir, my wife was placed on the floor. I had to pay for a bed."

"I paid," he said, dismissing it, annoyed.

"Sir, I can't work if my wife is not cared for."

"And I need front page news! You get the story and I will care for your wife."

I had to think of Shanti. I was a small boat again, tossed on a raging sea. And Mishra was the wave maker. He saw me relent, and he changed the direction of the wind.

"I'm not saying he should have been killed," he continued. "But Staines was into conversion. We both know it."

He was in no doubt that I would do as I was told.

"We just need some evidence. Account books - money in, money out, title deeds... Seek and ye shall find."

The message was clear. In my shock at what had happened, I had forgotten that my purpose was to expose Staines. That is what I was employed to do. While there was no longer any point in me trying to convert, my mission had not changed.

But I had.

I had seen a different perspective. I thought I had seen, and I still think this, I thought I had seen sincerity. And I had seen two small charred bodies. I sailed on, no longer caring as much about the waves.

"What about the boys?" I asked.

"His sons?"

"They killed them also."

Mishra took a moment to come to terms with this new revelation, I'll give him that. But he had no doubts about the rightness of his cause. All was interpreted through that absolute lens.

"They would have grown up to convert, like their father."

I think I was too shocked to say anything. I should have said, 'So they were killed for future crimes: possible future crimes.' How often we think of great things to say only after the event.

"We have to be strong, Banerjee," Mishra continued. "We have to print the truth. Staines was not a hero and not a martyr."

I risked one last manoeuvre. "Do you know a man named Mahendra?" I asked.

There was a moment, I am sure, but it was only a moment. Mishra was not a man to give anything away.

"No."

The meeting was over; the instructions clear. I made my way through the streets of Baripada to the Mission Compound. I have to remind myself now that I really knew very little about Staines at the time. Yes, my experience of him made me open to the possibility that I had been wrong about him, but those strongly held convictions about missionaries had not yet been dispelled. I believed Mishra was right and that I would still find evidence against Staines.

I don't know what I expected to find at the Mission, but certainly not the strange atmosphere that confronted me. There were people milling around everywhere. All sorts of people. From servants and nuns to town dignitaries and landowners. The Doctor was there. Rotary Club members mixed with villagers, drinking tea. A group was singing a hymn in the courtyard. A few were crying, but most just looked shocked, talking in low voices.

And most confronting of all... Gladys Staines, serving tea!

I didn't know what to make of it. Of course, I discovered later that Mrs Staines had not been told - she had received an early morning phone call to say that the vehicles had been burnt, but no further information.

But everybody else knew. Nobody saying anything. Nobody wanting to say anything. Everybody waiting for someone official to deliver the news.

As I wondered around the building - please don't judge me too harshly - I found an open door leading into a private ablution area, which in turn led to a bedroom. Surely, if there was evidence to be found, it would be found here. I entered the private bedroom of Graham Staines.

Yes, it seems insensitive, even to me. But remember, I was still certain that there would be some evidence, somewhere. Where else more likely than a private bedroom?

Nothing.

Nothing.

Nothing.

Actually, I did find some title deeds in a desk along with a number of personal letters. They were old. They were the original deeds issued by the King of Mayurbanj, granting the land they then occupied to the Leprosy Home.

And then, from a small table next to the double bed, I picked up a hardback copy of a book called *Jungle Pilot* about somebody with the surname 'Saint'. I forget the first name. I thought it an odd surname. It was about a missionary. It was about a missionary who had been killed for being a missionary.

I literally felt cold, my skin actually had the goosebumps. A story of a murdered missionary was the last book Graham Staines read... was reading... would never finish reading... I had seen enough.

But I do remember some lines from the book. They were underlined, so I scribbled them down in my pad.

"*Missionaries constantly face expendability and people who do not know the Lord ask why in the world we waste our lives as missionaries. They forget that they too are expending their lives.*"

These were the lines Graham Staines had underlined.

I slipped out of the room with a question that I still ponder: what will I have to show for the life I am expending?

I did not have time to ponder back then.

I had hardly left the room when I felt a sharp pain as I was driven against the wall, a solid wooden stick bruising against my ribs.

It was Pastor David.

Of course he was upset, but he was also a Christian pastor and I don't think violently attacking me was in keeping with that profession.

He wanted confirmation - what did I know? Nothing had been confirmed officially, which explained why Gladys Staines was still serving teas, hoping her husband and boys would arrive home at any moment. He also assumed I was involved, that I was the one inciting the violence; 'were you there?' he asked. He wanted someone to blame, someone to be angry with, anyone except his god.

He started to weep when I confirmed the deaths. Like most people, I think he had anticipated that Graham had been killed, but not the boys. Not the boys.

Even now I feel it and I say it... not the boys.

He began to weep, his anger dissipating.

"He must have done something," I said, echoing Mishra's words.

His anger returned tenfold. I suppose it was an ill-timed statement. He came at me with the stick, ready to strike. I got out of his way, fleeing to the relative safety of other people, hoping he would not pursue and make a scene. He let me go.

I was annoyed that he should be angry with me. I was as shocked as he at the murders. How dare he imply that it was my fault? I was still in denial that my words had anything to do with Mahendra's actions. And even if they did, this pastor could not have known what I had said.

I find it difficult, even now, to forgive the man completely, which makes what I am about to tell you even more stupendous.

The officials had arrived. Mrs Staines would be told the news no wife and mother ever wants to hear. I had not found evidence of fraudulent conversions, but at least I would have a first-hand account of her reaction. That had to be worth something. Grief might spill to anger, perhaps to curses and calls for justice, or even revenge.

I slipped into the house and positioned myself with a good view of Gladys Staines.

A well-dressed Indian lady approached her.

"Gladys," I heard her say, "I don't want you to be a stone. But you need to be strong for Esther."

She knew. Somehow she already knew, although she had obviously held onto the hope that she was wrong.

"You mean they're dead," she said.

It wasn't a question.

The news confirmed, Gladys Staines moved slowly, as if reaching to embrace someone; someone who wasn't there.

I don't believe she saw me, or anyone really. Yet it seemed to me that she looked directly at me.

"Whoever did this, we will forgive them," she said.

REVELATIONS AND AFTERMATH

Back in the marketplace when I first arrived in Baripada, I had heard the pastor, David, the one who had just tried to beat me, claiming that Christians should forgive their enemies. Not that he was doing this.

But here was someone who was.

Here was someone, in the most extreme of circumstances, when the senses must scream to do the opposite, claiming to offer that very thing: forgiveness to a vile and murderous enemy.

Of course, we should question the veracity of such a statement. She was in shock. Denial. Perhaps they were just words, unsupported by any real conviction. Some have since claimed it was only instinct.

But is that not all the more unexpected?

My instincts are nothing like these. Yet this woman's first reaction was... to forgive. Me. To forgive me. It mattered not that she didn't know the part I had played.

What would you do in that situation?

I would like to say I gave up my pursuit of evidence to condemn Staines, but I did not.

I walked from the compound in shock. Denial. It was not I who lit the torches, not I who crept deceptively in the dead of night upon sleeping innocence, not I who fuelled the fire, not I... not I...

But words have power.

So do words of forgiveness.

And her words only served to fuel my feelings of guilt.

I should have dropped my pursuit of evidence. But as Mishra had implied, I was young and inexperienced and foolish.

A large contingent from the Leprosy Home arrived as I was leaving. It was not usual for inmates to move beyond the confines of the Home, especially into the town. To come to the Mission Compound was an indication of the distress they were feeling.

They knew what had happened.

Many were crying openly.

They called him 'Dada', meaning father - a classic example of the worst kind of colonial paternalism is what I called it. "They have killed our father," one of them said.

I remembered then that leprosy was the 'veil' behind which Staines operated. And I had been warned, that I may need to have contact with lepers to find the evidence required to fulfil my mission.

I stalled at the Leprosy Home Gate.

To push through into that forbidden land, the metal bars of the gate standing like the entrance to a maximum security prison, within whose boundary only those with a life sentence should be admitted, the flaking paint of the cold metal sign like the flaking of lifeless, leprous skin, to push through, I felt, was indeed to take on a life sentence from which there may be no return.

I was right.

There is now no return, although at the time I did not know what that sentence was going to be. Of course, I cannot know - we never know - if this action was the one action that caused the consequence. The judgement may have been decided long since, perhaps even before coming to Baripada. But I will not speculate further, for such is the path to madness.

If this was where the evidence lay hidden, then this was where the nourishment for my garden of delight was to be found.

Some believe that the excrement of elevated beings, the higher castes, the Brahmin, provides the best fertilizer. But you have to be prepared to handle excrement.

The fertilizer I believed was needed lay beyond that gate. It was not the excrement of higher beings, but for me it was a form of excrement, entering the precinct of lepers. But here was the last possible place evidence might be found that would satisfy my employer, fertilizer needed to grow my journalism career, the risk I needed to take to provide for Shanti and Vardanuja.

The gate slid open easily.

It was eerily silent, the inmates having travelled to the Mission House at the news. I walked the long driveway nervously, not sure what to expect, or feel.

Was I being watched by silent eyes?

Was leprosy stalking me as I walked?

Foolish? Yes, but these are deep-seated fears.

I walked past cows and a small milking area. Nobody, unless you count the cows.

I walked past a clinic enclosed in wire mesh for treating the sick. I didn't stop.

I walked through a central work area with piles of *sabai* grass alongside woven mats and baskets, some left in mid weave, and various work implements... rice threshing had been underway when they had apparently left in a hurry.

And then, what I had been looking for. A door in the building on the far side with a faded label: 'Office'.

It was not locked. I took that to indicate how assured Staines had become that nobody would find him out, that nobody would come looking here, that he could act with impunity in this place.

A voice at the door shocked me out of my search.

"Looking for something?"

It was the old man, Sundar. The one who had caused me to lose my bus ride. The one I had refused to travel with in Staines' vehicle. The one, I now admit, who had paid for my bus ticket in the first place.

I struggled for composure. What was he still doing here?

He indicated to some files on a shelf, "The accounts ledger over there."

I went on the offensive.

"What did he give you to convert?"

"He's just been killed, yes?"

A nice avoidance of my question, but I was up to it.

"Yes, so you can tell me now - it doesn't matter anymore."

He said nothing. Just stared at me.

I was not going to back down. I kept up the pressure.

"Why did you convert?"

"You want the truth?" he asked.

Of course I did.

"Truth always seems to cost something," he said.

There it was.

I pulled the little money I had left from my pocket, trying to make it look more than it was. He showed no interest at that point, instead talking again.

"You know, from when I got leprosy to when Dada found me... in all those years, he was the only person who touched me."

I wondered where this was going.

"Is touching a leper an inducement?" he asked.

I didn't like where this was going.

And I was not going to let it go there. I moved quickly, stuffing my money back into my pocket, I was at him before he could move. Grabbing him by the shirt I shoved him up against the wall.

"Old man, I need to know what he offered you to convert!"

"You must be desperate to touch me."

"I want the truth about your conversion."

"Dada showed me God's love. Why wouldn't I convert?"

"So that you could stay here."

"I saw God's love..."

"He forced you. Say it!"

"I never converted!"

If a younger man had physically punched me it could not have stunned me more than that. I had assumed. I had seen him praying with Staines. I had depended on this being true.

He could see that I was struggling to assimilate his statement.

"The truth - I'm not a Christian. In 30 years he never forced me. Most people living here are not Christians. I never converted."

I asked a strange question then. I still don't know why I asked it. It came from somewhere deep within and surprised even me.

"Why not?"

As if to convert was the logical thing to do, in his situation anyway.

The old man's response was even more surprising.

"My son, I suppose."

The question and his admission must have touched a point of pain in his life. He kept talking, reflecting, perhaps realising for the first time...

"I always hope he will see me. But he cannot. He believes the lie that I'm dead."

He looked back at me.

"He's a newspaper editor now. Like you. He calls me the 'mad fool'."

If I had not been shocked by his revelations before, I most certainly was shaken up now. I had heard those words before, in Mishra's office, from his own mouth. Could it be?

"What is his name?" I asked.

"He changed his name," the old man said.

I didn't need to ask further. I knew.

For Mishra the damning of Staines was more than ideological; it was personal. Acceptance of Staines was acceptance of his hidden past, a cursed association that would cling to him more strongly than the disease itself, limiting him in every area of life.

Complete denial of his past was the only way to get ahead in a culture where, as Staines had said, even an educated man like me would not ride in the same vehicle as a man who had been cured of leprosy for thirty years.

How things had changed.

I walked from that office utterly beaten. I knew then, for certain, that I would not find the evidence I wanted. If I was to report the way Mishra wanted me to, I would have to speculate, allege, ignore, neglect... lie.

I wrote the article. My way. I wrote the facts as I saw them. I did not speculate. It was front page news and it was about murder, a black deed of cruelty that does not belong in a tolerant society.

Mishra was waiting for me. He had a deadline to make.

"What is this?" he asked as he surveyed the article.

"There's no evidence," I said.

"Nothing?"

"Nothing."

"Well, just write about the conversions for now."

"No."

That shocked him.

"It's not true," I said.

"Of course it's true - Staines has been converting for years."

"Not illegally."

"He converted. It is enough."

"To kill him? And his children?"

"The villagers are desperate..."

"That's not true."

"They have no voice. We have to be their voice."

I remember I lapsed into silence - he was starting to raise his voice.

"Think about your wife," he said.

Was it a threat? Was it blackmail? Or was it a genuine recommendation to do what I was being paid to do for the sake of my family?

"You just don't have the evidence yet," he continued. "I was young and idealistic once too. Let me help you."

Let me help you...

We are all faced with choices in our lives. How different my life might have been if I had let him. But would it have been better? No doubt, in some respects. But not in all. No, not in all.

The thing is, he was not just asking me to keep the report vague and imply Staines' guilt. I would be required to step over the line into falsely reporting that Staines was involved in illegal conversions. And given what has happened since - Justice Wadhwa's Commission of Enquiry and numerous arrests and convictions - it is not unlikely that I would have seen the inside of a jail cell for quite some time. I am certain that Mishra would have denied any knowledge of my lack of evidence.

At the time, of course, I was acting from instinct, reacting to the storm of emotion inside me as I tried to navigate out of the perfect storm Mishra had forged around me.

I took a step too far, or to continue my metaphor, I lowered my sails to be blown before by the blast of the storm.

"You can prove to me it's true, Sir," I said. "I just spoke to a man at the Leprosy Home who claims he has a son. A newspaper editor."

Mishra froze. I saw the blood drain from his face.

Why should he care this much, you may ask? People deny their relations all the time.

I can only tell you, and have told you, about my own deep-seated fear of leprosy. Mishra's denial was complete. I suppose his entire identity was established on the denial of his origins.

"Prove to me he's lying," I said. "Come and meet him."

"A leper."

"He's been healed."

"A convert and a liar."

"He never converted. He always hoped his son..."

"Raj!"

"Your father..."

"I have no father!"

The blood had risen again and he was nothing less than enraged. Suddenly, he grabbed my arm, pulling it toward him and turning his back to me, my arm gripped under his armpit, my hand in front of him.

I tried to resist but Raj gripped me from behind.

I didn't know what he was doing, although I soon found out. He clawed and ripped at the wedding ring until he had it from my finger.

"You want this," he said, holding up my ring, "you write my article the way I want it."

Then he added, partly to himself it seemed, but obviously intended for me, "Or I will call a certain 'father' who would love to get the man who seduced his daughter."

The perfect storm.

Raj threw me to the side - held as I was I had little chance to resist. Besides, he was a big man. Mishra was already in the car behind a locked door by the time I got back to my feet.

But this time it was I who was in shock. Mishra knew. I was no longer safe. Even if I wrote what he wanted I felt sure he would follow through with his threat. Because I also knew. About him.

I watched as Raj got behind the wheel and sped away.

I watched as individual pieces of paper emerged from the fleeing vehicle to be caught by the sudden wind, flicked into the air, and then float, deflated, at random back to earth.

I watched my notes, my research, interviews, thoughts, and draft articles, spread along the road as Mishra ripped my notebook apart, beyond the curve in the road, out of sight.

I let them go. I had a bigger problem to ponder now.

I didn't know there was worse to come.

Much worse.

But before I come to that... perhaps I am too afraid to type the words, to dredge the memories, to feel again... Nevertheless, I have come to the reason I type these words at all.

It was the book, you see, *Staines of India*, the book that I found in that bookshop in Kolkata. It was not just the book. It was the words.

My words.

In the book.

There they were, as I turned the pages, my research, my drafts, my notes, my true observations... the very words that Mishra had thrown to the wind to be blown from the sight of enquiring minds... here they were. In print.

Years later, admittedly, but here they were for all to see who cared to see.

The author, a journalist, explains how he found the first words in a page that was folded to hold a cone of peanuts he had purchased from a chai-walla.

He had paid the boy to provide as many of the pages as possible. And he had managed to salvage most of my notes.

Not once did a name appear with which he could track me, not that he would have found me.

So, here were my words, published, years later but still published, anonymously. The way I want it.

It is this victory, or vindication, that has me sitting once again at the typewriter.

And now I cannot avoid it any longer. I have to type the words I do not wish to type.

I returned to the hospital and tried to explain to Shanti the trouble I was in, that I needed to disappear, that her father was sure to look after her if she told him I had deserted her.

Ah, my Shanti... Shanti... well, she would not listen to reason. My reasoning, anyway.

She wanted to go with me.

That was impossible.

She wanted me to take Vardanuja.

Even more impossible.

She wanted me to stay.

I had little doubt now. That was to risk death.

But Shanti was afraid that if she threw herself on her father's mercy he would make her give up Vardanuja. And she would not risk it.

Tears flowed freely as she begged me, trying to come to terms with the situation.

It was in the midst of this intensity that I heard a sound behind me. Shanti gasped.

I turned to see Raj, Mishra's Raj, holding Vardanuja, a nervous nurse behind him.

Shanti was out of the bed before I had even turned back. Her instinct to love and protect was so strong. She didn't make it more than a few steps before she doubled over in pain.

We helped her back to the bed.

Clearly Mishra wanted his article. But it was more than that, wasn't it? He wanted to see me, the upstart who had dared to challenge the deception he had constructed, the worm who should have been his to command, he wanted to see me squirm and grovel and submit before he was done with me.

"The article for the child," I said.

Raj just stared at me.

I went to write Mishra's article.

I wonder what makes a man so... dead?

I wonder if that could have been me, had I made a different choice.

The article didn't take long to write. In exchange Raj handed me an old, large flat-bottomed bag. Vardanuja was safely asleep inside, resting in a pile of cloths, ready for travel. I wondered if it was a subtle hint from a man who had given over his life to Mishra.

I had to make a decision. Fast.

The Doctor met me as I entered the ward. I can still hear the words.

"She's in a coma."

The sudden movement had caused internal bleeding. There was no moving her now.

"What can I do? I asked.

"Pray," he said.

Pray.

I, who relied far more on my own abilities, I, who built up no credit with the gods, I, who had entered a leprosy home, touched a leper and spoken the words that led to the death of Graham, Philip and Timothy, I was not likely to be successful in prayer.

But I knew someone who may be successful and I was desperate enough to try.

Gladys Staines.

Can you believe my audacity?

Even more, can you believe that, in the midst of her grief, she made time for me? Yes, she did.

She was sitting on the floor in her boys' room when I was reluctantly ushered in to see her. She was touching their toys, gentle fingers, lovingly lifting, feeling...

"You say you need prayer?"

"Yes."

"I need prayer," she said.

"My wife is ill, in hospital, in a coma."

"Why do you think my prayers will be better than yours?"

I didn't answer. A person who could forgive, immediately, such as she had, was surely in close contact with the divine.

"Prayer's not magic," she said when I didn't answer. "What's your wife's name?"

"Shanti."

"Nice name."

She rolled onto her knees. The lady with her, a Hindu by the way, did the same. I followed, careful to do the same also.

I have this picture in my head. She was a tall woman by Indian standards anyway, yet she seemed so small, enveloped in a gentle sari, head bowed, hands folded, eyes closed... a picture of submission. Like that picture of Mother Teresa that I have, of humility kneeling, this time next to my pain, and also in pain.

"Heavenly Father, we ask your blessing and mercy on Shanti. If it's your will, Lord, please heal her. And may she and Manav know the peace that passes understanding, in the name of Jesus, the Christ. Amen."

I was taken by surprise at the simplicity. It was over so quickly. When I opened my eyes they were both looking at me.

"Is that all?" I asked.

"God's hearing is very good," she said.

Then the words that showed she was still human.

"But he may have other purposes than giving us what we want."

The words caught in her throat. She would not get what she wanted. The full realisation of grief had not yet come.

As I left, she asked if I had children.

"A daughter."

She handed me a small stuffed toy lamb.

"Perhaps she would like this."

It was her son's. How could I take it? How could I refuse such a gesture? Vardanuja still has it. It shares all her joys and sorrows.

But Gladys Staines was right. God does not always give us what we want.

I arrived at the hospital in time to see the nurses draw the sheet over Shanti's body.

EPILOGUE

I did one more thing before I disappeared with Vardanuja.

I returned to the house, stuffed essentials into a suitcase, and searched the bush nearby for a small wooden cross.

I found it.

It is a treasured possession that Vardanuja keeps, a symbol of hope, her mother's teeth marks still there in the wood.

I type these final words some months after I discovered *Staines of India* in that bookshop. In the six years since Graham, Philip and Timothy were murdered, and Gladys and Esther offered forgiveness, the conflict between Christians and non-Christians in many parts of India has increased.

Perhaps most is political; each side claims the other is the perpetrator. No doubt there is some truth in all of this. But the Christians seem to be getting the worst of it. They are certainly the minority. Of course, I am not there. I can only go by what I read, by what is reported, by what I might have written had I still been there.

But this I do know. While they were clearly far from perfect, and didn't claim to be, the Christ followers I met in Baripada were much more concerned about truth and following their Christ than about political power.

And that makes me wonder.

My daughter will always have a cross. Perhaps she will claim Jesus as her Christ some day. I will not object. I want her to have that freedom. I want her to not be fearful of such a choice.

Of course, I remain cautious, in many ways.

There is enough that is evil in the world. My name is not Manav, my daughter is not Vardanuja and I don't live in Kolkata.

Just in case.

THE MOVIE AND OTHER LINKS

If you haven't yet seen the film, starring Sharman Joshi, Stephen Baldwin and Shari Rigby, you may wish to do so. The following website should have information on where it can be accessed.

https://www.theleastofthese.movie/

Furthermore, starting with the film, a forgiveness movement has started up. You can find resources and stories of forgiveness, or share your own experiences at: https://iforgive.com/

A Message from Gladys Staines

Many of us have gone through trials and sufferings. But God knows what each one of us is going through.

Psalm 46:1 says, "God is our refuge and strength, an ever-present help in trouble."

God is the one who encourages us and strengthens us to forgive. In the midst of heartache and sorrow – forgiveness enables us to look to the future. Unforgiveness brings bitterness which affects our health and relationships.

Jesus taught us to forgive. But forgiveness doesn't take away all the consequences for the victim or the perpetrator. Because Jesus lives I can face tomorrow. All fear is gone. Because I know God holds the future.

- December 2018